How to Publish Your Poetry

The First-Ever Marketing Manual and Success Guide for Poets

by Thomas A. Williams, Ph.D.

An Info-Pak® Book

Venture Press
Washington, NC
104 South Respess Street
(919) 975-2066

Books by Thomas A. Williams

Mallarme and the Language of Mysticism
Eliphas Levi: Master of Occultism
We Choose America
Tales of the Tobacco Country
The Bicentennial Book
How to Make $100,000 a Year in Desktop Publishing
The Self-Publisher's Handbook: Contacts and Sources
How to Make Money Publishing Real Estate Guides

Special Reports

The Query Letter That Never Fails
How to Write a Living Family History
The Article Format That Always Sells
Ten Books You Can Write and Publish for Pleasure and for Profit

·

Table of Contents

*This book is dedicated to my
daughter and partner in publishing,
Lisa Christina Williams.*

Chapter 1

*You **Can** Publish Your Poetry*

Do you want to become a published poet? The chapters in this book will tell you, step-by-step, what you must do to achieve this sought-after goal. The author is a magazine and book publisher who has evaluated poetry submissions day after day for many years. Some he has purchased for publication. Most he has returned to those who wrote them.

Why are some poems read and accepted? Why are others rejected and returned? Is there anything that a poet who is serious about publication can do to make sure that *his* poems are among those that get into print?

Happily, there is a great deal that can be done, and it will work. Read and reread this book. Absorb the information it contains. Absorb every detail. Put the techniques it describes to work for you. Get into action not only as a poet but as a seller of poems. Non-fiction writers actively market their work, and they get published. You, as a poet, must utilize the same techniques that they do, adapted to your needs.

The pages which follow contain an organized approach to the marketing of poetry that anyone can adopt and follow. When you do you will be amazed at the results. You will see your work in print, regularly, and in the places where you want it to be. And you will learn what you need to know to build a successful career

"Nobody, I hope, will accuse me of conceit in these opinions of mine own capacity of doing great things. In good truth, I think the word suffers from this much-bepraised modesty. Who should be a better judge of a man's talents than himself? . . . Yes, I would write a book? And who should say that it might not be a very pretty book? Who knows but that I might do something very respectable?"

—Walt Whitman

as a poet.

- You will learn methods that will help you place your poems in magazines and other periodicals regularly.

- You will learn how to interest publishers in bringing out your poems in book form.

- You will learn how to sell these books once they are published.

- You will learn how to enhance your reputation as a published poet to achieve worthwhile goals.

- You will learn how to successfully self-publish and market your work for yourself.

- You will even learn how to set up your own small publishing company to publish the work of other poets as editor of your own poetry series.

Two Poetical Facts of Life

There are two inescapable facts of life that every poet must deal with. The first is the difficulty of writing the poem itself. Getting the words right, the images right, the rhythms right can be an almost overwhelming task. And the better the poet the more difficult the task becomes. It is no easy thing to give true utterance to the deepest parts of one's personal vision.

This is the poet's first inescapable fact of life.

The Second Fact: You've Got To Find A Publisher

Yet, in spite the obstacles that stand in their way, poets do manage to write poems that satisfy them. But that which is written is meant to be read. The life cycle of a poem is not complete until it is published—made public—and made available to the sympathetic reader. At this point the poet faces the second inescapable fact of life: nothing is seemingly harder for any writer than to find a publisher for a poem.

Fortunately, the key word in that last sentence is "seemingly." For my experience as editor and publisher tells me that the good poet who will market his or her work systematically and thorough-

Notes

ly can succeed in getting published and do so far more frequently and happily than anyone would ever suspect.

You may even—wonder of wonders—succeed financially, earning modest amounts of money directly from the sale of your books and indirectly from opportunities as speaker, teacher and consultant that will become open to you as a published poet.

Learn from Your Non-Fiction Brethren

A successful writer of non-fiction magazine articles understands from the beginning that to be a good writer is not enough. He understands that, in addition to mastering the craft of writing, he has to learn to market his work. He carefully and painstakingly studies market trends and needs. He masters the art of writing query letters and book outlines. He establishes a specialty and cultivates a group of magazines and magazine editors who are interested in the kind of thing that he has to say.

To the degree that he is successful he will have learned to be persistent. He doesn't stop trying to sell an article idea until he has *systematically exhausted all publication possibilities.* He understands that sooner or later, if he just keeps at it, there will be fortuitous matching of his idea and a publisher's immediate need. And when that happens the result is very happy indeed: publication and a check in the mail.

Self-Publication: A Publishing Revolution

When the non-fiction writer is dealing with a book idea rather than an article idea he follows the same course.

If, after approaching all likely publishers, he is unable to find one who both likes and needs the book he has to offer he may very well *publish it himself.* He understands that because of the new technology of desk-top publishing, fax machines and telecommunications there has been an absolute revolution in the publishing business. As the big publishing houses founder, the independent presses—often one or two person shops—are thriving, and he has no hesitation at all in joining this wave of change and progress.

Poets Take Note

Poets who use these same techniques and adopt these same attitudes can and will be published, too. Yet very few seem to do so. The feeling that the systematic selling of one's product is somehow

---

Notes

"Any writer overwhelmingly honest about pleasing himself is almost sure to please others."

—*Maryanne Moore*

Notes

beneath the attention of the poet is a dreadfully self-defeating one.

It certainly is not one shared by some very great poets. Walt Whitman, the greatest American poet of them all, was a tireless self-promoter. The famous public readings given in our own day by such poets as Dylan Thomas were not only literary events but masterpieces of promotion and marketing. They generated newspaper articles and stories and accounted for a generous portion of the sales of his books. Thomas was a very fine poet, but it was the marketing of his work as much as the quality of it that made it sell to such a wide public.

Allen Ginsburg, whose poem "Howl" was one of the most important of his generation, became widely read due in large part to his unique gift for self-promotion. The powerful public persona he created for himself produced thousands of pages of newspaper, magazine and book copy. The great success of this one poem became the cornerstone of an entire career.

Not all self-marketing is as flamboyant and aggressive as that of Ginsburg. It must, after all, grow out of the personality of the poet. Quite impressive regional reputations have been built on the simple willingness of poets to seek and fulfill assignments as "poets in the schools", to give readings at community colleges, appear on local talk shows and achieve and maintain high visibility in regional arts and literary organizations.

Opportunity Doesn't Knock. You Do.

To do any of these things you can't sit back and wait for opportunity to come to you. You have to go to it. If the opportunity to publish your poetry is what you want, you have to locate it, seek it out, confidently approach it and beat the door down, if necessary, until the way is clear.

In his classic success manual, *Think and Grow Rich*, Napoleon Hill tells how, as a young man, he got the job he set his mind on. "I applied in the regular way," he recalls, "and didn't get hired. I then sent a follow-up letter every week for four weeks. When that failed I sent a letter every day. Finally I sent a telegram every hour on the hour for two days. At the end of this time I got a call. 'Come on in to work,' the voice said. 'We give up. The job is yours.'"

While I do not recommend this degree of overkill in approaching editors—who will not have the time to deal with all these inquiries—*it is essential to develop a marketing plan appropriate to your goal of getting your poetry published and implement it relentlessly.* In the end it will pay off for you.

There are many opportunities to publish poetry. But only those that you identify and approach in the professional, persistent, don't-take-no-for-an-answer ways described in this book are likely to get the results you desire.

Notes

Chapter 2

What Every Poet Should Know about the Economics of Publishing.

What is going on in the offices and in the mind of the publisher or editor on whose desk the postman deposits your packet of poems? The answer to this question is basic to your strategy, and to help you understand it I hereby offer this *Poet's Short Course in the Economics of Publishing.*

Until you truly comprehend and accept the facts presented in this chapter, you will be like a player who has devoted his life to winning a game of whose rules he is totally ignorant. And that, my friends, is what is known as a handicap.

So that you will not suffer from a similar handicap in your efforts to break into print, you must first understand—and understand very clearly—that publishing is a business. Like the professional in any other business, the goal of the publisher is to make a profit. People who work as publishers use these profits to buy groceries, pay the rent and send the children off to college, just like the rest of us. They also use these profits to publish more books like yours.

"There are generally two sides to magazine organization. Purely business aspects are the responsibility of a publisher and her staff. This includes...all the details that keep a magazine from going broke....All the non-advertising content of the magazine is in the hands of the editors....Most (editors) are harried, hassled and constantly battling deadlines."

—Franklynn Peterson and Judi Kesselman-Turkel, in The Magazine Writer's Handbook.

A Risky Business

Publishing is also a risky business. Pitfalls and dangers beset the unwary publisher on every side. The opportunity for financial loss is every bit as great—and usually greater—that the chance of gain.

The successful publisher truly lives by his wits. He guesses which books are likely to find favor with the reading public, and he publishes them. He decides which articles are likely to interest the readers of his magazine and he buys them. He is often on the lookout for specialty items—including poems—*that will be meaningful to his specific readership* and he buys these too.

In making these decisions the publisher/editor relies on his intuition and experience. If he misjudges too often, there is no profit, no groceries, no rent, no college tuition for the kids. Hence, since no one can afford to stay in a business that doesn't bring in enough money to live on, there is no longer a publisher.

Those Free Enterprise Twins: Risk and Profit

The free enterprise system is built on the twin pillars of risk and profit. You risk what you have—money, time, talent— in the hope of gaining far more than you risk. But it doesn't always work. In this way it is a little like a loaded shotgun. The trusty, old double-barrel can be used to hunt for game and stock the family larder. But misjudge a step and stumble, and that same reliable tool can shoot your foot off.

I go into all this so that you, as a poet, can put yourself for a moment into the editor's or publisher's shoes. For them, everything is always at risk. As they practice their profession they stand to make a profit. But they also may shoot themselves in the foot. This smarts, and most publishers will do everything they can to avoid it.

Most of us literary types don't really understand—or perhaps just don't think about—the risk/profit basis of business in general and the publishing business in particular. Before I became a publisher I was a college professor. If I taught well, there was a check at the end of the month. If I taught badly, there was a check at the end of the month. When I didn't teach all summer long there was *still* a check at the end of the month. My financial reward for the work I had done was not directly related to the level of success I had achieved in it. The good fairy might as well have put my money in the departmental mailbox.

Notes

And then....I resigned my tenured professorship to become a publisher.

It was quite a revelation, as abrupt and sudden a reality bath as anyone has ever taken. When I performed badly, I got no check. The good fairy had taken a permanent leave of absence. Moreover, I had to pay out some of the money I had already received to cover current overhead and keep the doors open. If I took time off, I did not get paid. And no matter how well business was going at any given time, there lurked in the background the cold, sobering all-too-true knowledge that things could (and would) go awry whenever they took a notion to do so. A book could bomb. Subscriptions could fall off. Postal rates could rise and eat up my profits. A competitor could come into the arena and dilute my market share ruinously. Or my building could burn down, or I could have a heart attack and not be able to continue in business.

Obviously I was betting that more good things than bad would happen to me and, on balance, this has been true. But it took constant attention and alertness to market opportunities and danger signals to bring this result about. Even in the best of times I was—and still am—constantly aware that every decision I make about what I accept for publication affects me and my business directly, as well as the well-being of those who depend on me. Except, perhaps, in the largest corporations, where responsibilities may be more diffuse or camouflaged, these basic human realities constitute the everyday furnishings of every editor's office, right along with the desk, the chair and the word-processor.

And it is into this office that your poems arrive, unsolicited.

Most of the magazines, journals, chapbooks and other periodicals that publish poetry are brought out by relatively small companies that, in order to stay in business, must watch their finances closely.

But they are not the only ones at risk. Bigger fish than they are in harm's way as well. Just three years ago, at a meeting of the North Carolina Writer's Network, I heard an enthusiastic young editor/ publisher describe the start-up that he was then involved in. He gave us a detailed plan for the publication of *Southern Magazine*. The idea was that a magazine with a focus on the South and with a new-journalism style and an aggressive editorial policy, a la *Texas Monthly* or *Esquire*, would generate subscriptions and advertising sales sufficient to turn a profit. The project was not underfinanced. There was five million dollars in operating capital in the bank.

Southern Magazine appeared. It was well-designed and edited.

Notes

"Books of Poetry can sell, but these sales are almost totally dependent on the reputation, personality and contacts of the poet....If your poet is not outgoing enough to do well at a public reading and not aggressive enough to arrange a regular schedule of them, the book will not sell."

—*Thomas A. Williams,*
in How to Make
$100,000 a Year in
Desktop Publishing.

Notes

The articles in it were first rate. Yet within three years the project ran out of gas. The five million was gone, and advertising revenues were not producing adequate cash flow to produce the hoped-for profit. The originating editor's name disappeared from the masthead. The magazine was sold to another company and its name and character were changed.

Publishing Magazines: A Financial Tightrope Act

Profits are slim in the magazine business. Most operate on the tiniest of profit margins. They barely manage to produce the positive cash flow that enables them to stay in business. And even this is often accomplished by paying editors, artists and writers (as you well know) as little money as possible.

Subscription and single copy (newsstand) sales do not return a profit. Selling subscriptions by mail is expensive. Few readers renew their subscriptions automatically. To get them to do so requires an additional series of mailings. In fact, cash received from subscription sales and newsstand sales is barely adequate to support the cost of subscriber maintenance and the high cost of mailing out the magazines themselves.

Thus, when the editor reads through your submissions he will have very important questions in his mind in addition to the one about the quality of your writing. Assuming that your poem is well written, he will ask himself such questions as these:

• Will my readers understand this poem?

• Will my readers like this poem and react positively to it?

• Will this poem pull its weight in creating positive reader reactions to my magazine?

• Is its subject matter in keeping with the editorial slant of my magazine?

• Is it short enough to fit easily into available fill space?

• Is the poet someone whose name my readers will recognize and react positively to?

• Can I do more for my magazine by using this poem than I can by putting something else in the same space?

Such non-literary questions as these provide the background for the editor's evaluation and largely determine whether he stuffs your piece in the SASE you provided and returns it to you or whether he keeps it for further consideration or even accepts it for publication.

In the case of acceptance the poet *still* faces the obstacle of getting into the magazine on a timely basis. Space is expensive. The poem can be used only *as space permits and when space permits.*

The Book Publishing Business

It is difficult under any circumstances for an unknown poet to find a publisher for a book of verse. Without requisite marketing skills and a clear understanding of the economics of book publishing, it is virtually impossible. The reason is simple. With very few exceptions books of poetry seldom make any money.

Here's the way book publishing works. The publisher brings out a paperback book of verse. He can sell it, at the most, for $10. Since he has learned that even the best verse does not sell very well, he has printed no more than 1000 copies and very likely—especially in the case of small presses—just 500. This means that he does not realize any economy of scale in the manufacture of is books. The production cost per copy of the book is relatively high.

If the publisher knows his stuff and gets the best prices available, he can get the 500 copies printed and bound for, say, $1500, or $3 a book. He will have paid a typesetter 300 or so dollars. He has paid someone to paste the book up and ready it for printing. He has office overhead, billing expenses and distribution expense. An artist will earn an additional $200 for a cover design. The publisher then pays the bookstores and wholesalers who sell his book at least 50% of the cover price and sometimes more.

In all, if he sells every copy available to him for sale (450, since 50 will have been mailed out for review) he will gross $4500.

- Of that $4500 he pays his retailers their 50% discount, leaving him $2250.

- Of that $2250 he will lose $250 to bad debts and spoilage, leaving $2000.

- Yet he has paid the printer $1500, the typesetter $300, the cover artist $200. He will allow 10% of the gross for general office expense and overhead. All of this totals $2450.

Notes

The result: in the best of all possible worlds the publisher *loses* $450 on a book of poems that successfully sells every available copy of the first edition.

So why do some books of verse get published in spite of these facts?

- Sometimes the publisher is publicly supported, as is the case with a university press.

- Sometimes the publisher, who has other projects on which he is making money, brings out a book of verse for the love of it. I have done this myself. But you, as a poet, can't count on it. It doesn't happen every day.

- Sometimes (and this is more and more often the case, even with small presses of high reputation) the poet contributes to the expense of publication.

- Sometimes the poet has a known reputation for giving successful readings and for self-promotion, thereby convincing the publisher that an edition of a thousand or more copies can be sold so that he can at least break even on the project.

You Can Beat The Odds

And please bear in mind that all the while the publisher is expending his time and energy on your book of poems he is *not* doing the all the other things on which he depends for his livelihood.

These are the facts. You ignore them at your peril. If you think that they stack the odds against you, you are absolutely right. That's the bad news.

The good news is that these odds can be beaten when you understand them and take steps to deal with them. The remaining chapters will tell you how it is done.

Notes

Chapter 3

Nine Secrets of Publishable Poetry

Let's begin by asking a simple question. From an editor's point of view, what makes poetry publishable?

It is tempting to say that poetry that is very, very good and very powerful is publishable, but that may not necessarily be the case. It *is* true that the very best poems written are *worthy* of publication and *ought to be* published. But it does not follow that they *will* be published.

The history of literature is filled with the names of great poets who had great difficulty getting their work before the public. Of course, we only know the names of those who ultimately succeeded in doing so. One wonders how many Emily Dickenson's and Gerard Manly Hopkinses there are whose work never did see the light of day.

Those who write at the highest level of achievement in every genre are exceedingly rare. Not every American novelist is a Faulkner or a Hemingway. The rest of us must study the available market for novels and poems slant our production toward it. A survey of the field will quickly reveal the kinds of subject matter, style and treatment that promise success.

As editor and publisher of a regional magazine and owner of

Notes

Where do ideas come from? They are all around us and in us, if we would just pay attention to them and harvest them. The mind— your mind, my mind—is constantly emitting ideas, images, entire lines, even. These are what the great French poet Paul Valery used to call "vers donnees"—ready-made lines. Often these ideas and images represent the best that our creative minds are capable of. Keep a notebook with you at all times. Capture these random thoughts in your notebook. Like a spark caught up in tinder, unimaginable heat and light may grow from them later. Thoughts that you do not capture are lost forever. This is what I call "mind-harvesting", and it is essential.

an independent book publishing company I have read many submissions by poets anxious for publication. Some of these submissions I accepted, even though my magazine did not normally use
poetry. Most I returned to the author with thanks and a notice of
rejection that was as kind and thoughtful as I could make it.

Sometimes good work was returned to the author because
there was simply no room for it in the foreseeable future. More
often it was returned because the poems *did not embody all or most
of the nine characteristics that would have made them publishable in a
magazine or periodical of general circulation.*

Check you own work against the list provided here. The more
of these publishing secrets you master and incorporate into your
work the more effectively you will be able to stake your claim to
the limited space that is available at any given time.

1. **Your Poem Must Be Accessible to the General Reader.** The
   editor who is evaluating your poem will ask himself: will my
   readers understand and appreciate this verse? If there is any
   question at all in his mind, your work will be returned to you
   with a rejection slip.

The more clear and direct your work is the more likely it is to
be accepted. As an editor I often enjoyed poems submitted to me
that were rendered less than publishable by the obscure personal
references they contained—allusions to events or persons important to the poet but unlikely to be recognized or appreciated by
others.

This is a more general problem than you may think, and a
couple of examples may be in order. I had an uncle who was very
important to me as I was growing up. He was a backwoodsman
and always wore a peculiarly floppy, wide-brimmed felt hat. This
hat was unlike that worn by any other member of the family, and
to this day I identify him with it. Nevertheless, I could scarcely expect a reader to understand my feelings if the floppy hat appeared
in my poem as a passing reference with no explanation and no
uncle beneath it.

Such private symbols, for all the power they may exert on us
personally, cannot be understood by others. The public use of
wholly private symbolism just does not work. Art itself may very
well exist as a wholly private enterprise, but successful art, with
its goal of communicating our vision to as many of our fellow men
as possible, is always public.

I once wrote a poem that was built around another powerful
image from my childhood. I had stood on the back porch of our

Notes

18

South Georgia farmhouse and watched while my mother vainly struggled to keep a weeping willow tree safe as a hurricane passed nearby. The harder she fought the more apparent it became to me that she would fail. And she did.

This little drama came to embody for me the feeling that we are always at the mercy of forces far greater than our power to withstand them and to which we must always give in. The poem failed, of course, because this association with willows was wholly personal. The mere mention of the willow could not possibly engender in others the same strong feelings as it did in me.

Many poems are made virtually inaccessible to the general reader by the number of intellectual, literary and philosophical allusions they contain. I have observed that poets who are also college teachers often fall into this kind of poetical self-indulgence. Either they are simply writing for each other—a very restricted readership indeed—or they are writing private verses for their private pleasure.

It takes a very great and very powerful poet to get away with such obscurities. And even in those cases we read the works they create not because of the obscurities but in spite of them.

It was the unmistakable power of the opening lines of Eliot's *The Waste Land* that made the chore of dealing with the literary and anthropological puzzles in the remainder of the text worthwhile and even necessary for me.

Fortunately, it is possible to write poetry of the very highest quality that is readily accessible to the general reader, although it may contain level upon level of deeper and deeper meaning. I think of such diverse poets as Dante, Francois Villon, Charles Baudelaire and Robert Frost.

This is certainly not whimpy poetry. It is readily accessible to any reader that comes upon it. The door to it is easily opened— although, once inside, not every reader will explore or be capable of exploring every room, every nook and cranny from attic to basement.

When I was a boy I thought *Birches* was a poem about ice storms, and I was very satisfied with it that way. I read Dante almost as science fiction or fantasy. But I did read these poems and poets, and I profited enormously thereby as I grew and explored more and more of the hidden places of meaning they contained. The important thing, though, was that even on the twelve-year-old level these great poems were accessible. Always keep in mind that to be accessible does not mean to be superficial—a fact that can be very reassuring.

Notes

"The way to reach the better-paying magazines is by studying them just as thoroughly as a farmer studies the food market before he decides which crops to plant. That's why the first thing we're going to teach you...is a thorough understanding of the marketplace."

—Franklynn Peterson and Judi Kesselman-Turkel, in The Magazine Writer's Handbook.

2. **Your Poem Must Deal With a Broadly Shared Human Experience.** It's a free country. You can write about whatever you want to write about. But if you want to publish the poems that you write you should deal with broadly shared human experiences, and the more broadly shared the better.

Love is a broadly shared experience. Necrophilia is not.

Anxiety is a broadly shared experience. The details of your personal bankruptcy are not. And so on.

I think that most of us tend to recognize in ourselves and in others feelings, needs, compulsions that we all have in common, so this may be an easy requirement to satisfy. We simply have to be careful not to let the shared quality become submerged and hidden in the part of it that is personal with us alone.

Billie Varner is a North Carolina poet whose work I was instrumental in publishing. She writes about the simple relationships in her life, and she does so in a way that we can all immediately recognize as *our* experience, not simply the pains and pleasures of Billie Varner. Billie published her first book, *Come Share My World With Me* when she was in her sixties. She has since published two more volumes, all of which sold out the initial printing. She is currently preparing her *Collected Poems,* which my company will publish in the fall of 1990.

Billie Varner is no academician. Literary devices and artifices are foreign to her. She has wonderfully immediate access to her feelings and to the world around her. Her great success stems wholly from the fact that in her simple, lucid and unpretentious verse she taps directly into the vast and infinite well of shared human experience.

3. **Your poem should treat a subject for which there is a market.** I can hear the disgruntled mumblings, now. "Poetry is above such mundane considerations," you may be saying. To which I reply, "Not for the poet who wants to be published, and published regularly. "

Even the most high-browed, allusion-prone of the academic poets writes for a market. He writes for journal editors who are on the lookout for others who share their (often unconscious but nonetheless real) abstract and literary view of life. They tend to experience life as strained through the sieve of the literary tradition, discarding all that doesn't seep through. Such a poet, intensely aware of the needs of the market he is aiming for, would not dream of sending a simple rhyme about, say, his daughter's first date into the rarefied atmosphere of one of these journals. His submission

---

Notes

"It is true that the poet does not directly address his neighbors; but he does address a great congress of persons who dwell at the back of his mind, a congress of all those who have taught him and whom he has admired; they constitute his ideal audience and his better self. To this congress the poet speaks not of peculiar and personal things, but of what in himself is most common, most anonymous, most fundamental, most true of all men...."

—*Richard Wilbur*

would be rejected. The poetry might be good, but the subject matter would not be right for the periodical in question.

Some examples of marketable topics? Christian and other inspirational themes find a warm reception these days in many publications. There are scores of denominational magazines, newspapers and newsletters hungry for such material, and their editors will be pleased to hear from you. These publications offer happy hunting grounds for the poet still trying to break into print. If the subject matter is right and the poem well-written to boot, then you stand a very good chance of getting a serious reading. Best of all, once you're in, repeat publication of other poems becomes a real possibility.

I have said that I edited and published a regional magazine. This was *Tar Heel: The Magazine of North Carolina,* a slick paper, full-color state magazine. It was heavily slanted toward lifestyle, historical-nostalgia and tourism kinds of material. I did not advertise that I would publish poetry, but whenever I received a sheaf of poems from a writer I always read them with interest.

Some of these, I found, were very well written, but I couldn't use them. The subject matter was wrong. I needed poems about people, places and events immediately recognizable to my readers. That is to say, the poems needed a bit of local color, and that local color had to be Carolinian or at least compatible with North Carolina people and places. In style the verse had to be accessible. Within those limits I chose the very best of what was submitted to me, and I am happy to say that I was able to publish some very good work indeed. But first, the *subject matter* had to be right.

My magazine was not the only publication catering to this same readership. There was *The State* magazine and *We the People of North Carolina* as well as assorted lesser ones. In addition there were multi-state but still regional magazines like *Mid-Atlantic Country* and, in South Carolina, *Sandlapper.*

An enterprising poet could have seen that there was indeed a market for the kind of poetry I was accepting at *Tar Heel* and slanted his work toward it. The same pieces might also have been adapted for similar magazines in other states, as well.

The poet, to be happily and consistently published, must learn from the non-fiction free-lancer. He must analyze the markets, define the markets and write poems with subject matter appropriate to them. Or, at the very least, after having written a poem, analyze the markets to see where to send it. My experience is that the first alternative is much more likely to produce success.

4. **Your poetry should, whenever possible, be timely.** Publish-

Notes

able poetry is timely poetry. This is true in a general sense and in a particular sense. In the general sense publishable poems, if they are time-sensitive at all, relate to events, concerns, conflicts or movements that many people share, and they are submitted at the time of this sharing.

Delay in submitting timely material can be fatal to publication possibilities. I recently received a manuscript from a public school teacher who had been in Berkeley during the early days of the free speech-anti war movement of the sixties. She had gone there from a small southern town where she had spent her entire life up to that time. The culture shock was enormous, and she told about it in an engaging, personal way.

Her work was good. At an earlier period—when it was still timely—I might have been tempted to publish it. However, by the time the author had pulled it out of her files and mailed it off to me some twenty-five years had passed. The themes were dated, the personal reactions and contradictions she described no longer vital for a new generation of readers. The material, as well-written as it was, was old hat.

Perhaps you want to write a basically untimely poem because it is important to you to do so, or because you consider the subject intrinsically "worth" the effort. And you may be absolutely right. Nevertheless it is a fact that lack of timeliness will make your poem far less likely to find its way into print that would otherwise be the case.

In the particular sense timeliness leads to the production of occasional verse—poetry tied to a holiday or other occasion. Christmas poems get published at Christmas, patriotic poems at the Fourth of July, sweetheart poems at St. Valentine's day. And they are published widely, in newspapers, magazines, newsletters and every other possible kind of printed and readable product.

If you wish to submit occasional verse, do so several months in advance. Christmas poems should be sent out in late summer, Independence Day verse in January or February. You submit early not only because editorial decisions are made far in advance of publication. You also want to allow yourself time to get your poem back in the case of a rejection and resubmit it elsewhere before it is too late.

5. **Publishable poems are of manageable length**. Even those editors who love poetry and do whatever they can to support poets and publish their work face very real space problems. Publishing is a business. Space is expensive. Every item published must pay its way.

Notes

When the editor of a magazine does find a poem that he likes and wants to publish, he must find a place for it. If the poem is too long, he simply will not accept it, knowing that he will never have adequate space at his disposal.

How long is too long? I would say that a poem is unlikely to find a ready market in a general interest magazine if it runs longer that one-third of a magazine page. The rule is that in poetry less is better. A one-sixth page poem will be even more easily published. Verse requiring two-thirds of a page or more is unlikely to find a home in the consumer magazine market.

In a sense, poetry is treated almost as filler. It is used when there is "left over" space at the end of an article and when no advertising has been sold to fill that space.

6. **Publishable poems, especially those published in book form, are thematically related.** In the magazine market you can gradually build a market for yourself when you become known for producing good verse on a particular theme.

This is especially true for poets who write humorous verse. An example would be the word-play verses written by Willard Espy and published monthly in *Writer's Digest*. Espy has carved out a niche for himself. He has built up a faithful following that editors can rely on.

Other specialties? Erma Bombeck has built a following for her wry observations on family life and relationships. Poems in the same humorous and insightful vein might build a reputation and find ready reception for anyone capable of writing them.

Other themes will occur to you, growing out of your own experience. Once an editor accepts your work and finds that his readers like it he will be open to other pieces of the same type. In this way an acceptance becomes the beginning of an on-going relationship rather than an one-time stand.

7. **Thematically related poems make publishable books**. I have a formula that has served me well in testing book ideas for success. In is this: *Books can be profitably published and sold when they appeal to a large number of readers in a limited geographical area.* When a publication meets these criteria I know that I can sell it. There are many buyers and they are concentrated in an area that I can cover without a national sales organization.

City magazines, city and county histories and many other publications fall into this category, and the independent publisher who knows how to bring them out can make money thereby. (These

Notes

"Modern poets talk against business, but all of us write for money. Beginners are subjected to trial by market, poor things."

—*Robert Frost*

ideas are fully developed in my book *How to Make $100,000 a Year in Desktop Publishing*, published by Betterway Publications in 1990. For ordering information see the appendix.)

Poets can use the same criteria for testing ideas for books of verse. I recently published a book of poems by North Carolina poet Joseph Bathanti. It was work of the highest quality, with no concession whatsoever to the merely commercial. Just very good poems by a very good poet—a book that I was quite proud to be associated with as publisher.

Two things made me believe that I could sell enough of Bathanti's books to at least break even on the project. The first of these was the fact that the poems had all been written in and about the land and people of a North Carolina county. *They were thematically related. I knew I would be able to sell quite a few copies of the book, Anson County,* in the county itself. I also knew that all North Carolina libraries would be good prospects for buying a copy. As a matter of fact the Anson County Development Commission, within a few weeks of publication, bought enough copies to defray over half of the out-of-pocket production costs.

I think that "Outer Banks Poems", or "Savannah in Verse", or "Visions of Atlanta" would sell as well—at least well enough to recover costs and make a modest profit.

The related themes need not be geographical, although the marketing problems become more difficult when they are not.

The second reason I knew that I could afford to publish *Anson County*, by the way, was that I knew the poet to be a very good reader of his work, an active presenter. Few books of poetry are sold in bookstores. Most are sold at readings or at other special occasions where they can be sold and signed by the poet himself. Joe Bathanti, by virtue of his talent and energy, was a self-promoter. It was he who sold the first $1000 dollars worth of books to the county development people.

8. **The market-sensitive poet strives to create personal, public visibility. The poems that he writes thereby become more publishable**. It is not good enough to *be* a poet. If you want to get published it helps to be *known* as a poet.

Among my friends are writers who, though no better and no worse than many others, always seem to be getting into print, especially in state and regional anthologies and collections as well as in area literary publications, newspapers and magazines. They are able to do this because they have created a public visibility for themselves, at least among the limited group of individuals who

	Notes

control these publications. They join writer's groups, apply for grants, give talks. They serve on editorial boards and arts council boards. Often they get themselves into the position of being one of those instrumental in awarding grants—a very strong position indeed.

They are everywhere, all the time, in the arts community of their region. Consequently they get published when others don't. They give public readings and speeches at the drop of a hat. They organize "poets in the schools" programs, participate in writer's conferences, lead seminars, talk to every group that will have them.

Such poets are far more likely than others to have a *book* of their poems brought out. If publishing a book of your poetry is your ultimate goal, then developing this kind of public visibility is essential for success.

More on this important topic in the chapter devoted to self-promotion.

9. **Publishable Poems Are Well-Crafted Poems**. You *knew* I would get to this point, didn't you. No matter how much attention you pay to the marketing and purely commercial aspects of you work as a writer, the poems you submit must reflect your very best efforts at the poet's craft. There are very few—if any—new ideas, and probably no really new human experiences. What makes a poem is not so much *what* you talk about as *how* you talk about it.

A young writer once asked the great French poet Stephane Mallarme where he got ideas for his poems. "My dear fellow", Mallarme replied, "you don't make poems with ideas. You make them with words." It is the writer's craft, the powerful play of words, rhythms and images, that transforms a feeling or a thought into a poem.

Always keep at it until you get it right. Don't be satisfied with anything less than your best. Don't leave a kink in a line that you haven't taken time to smooth out. Don't use the almost right image when you know the right one is lurking somewhere in the shadows of your mind.

Remember Mark Twain's marvelous admonition the for the writer. The difference, Twain said, between the almost right word and the right word is the difference between the lightening bug and the lightening.

SUBMISSIONS RECORD

Publication	Editor	Date Sent	Returned	Comments
1.				
2.				
3.				
4				
5				
6				
7				
8				
9				
10				
11				
12				
13				
14				
15				
16				

Chapter 4

How to Publish Your Poems in Magazines

My years as editor of a regional magazine and a small book publishing company have taught me that the vast majority of queries and submissions of fiction, non-fiction and poetry alike that arrive each morning on the editor's desk are so unprofessional in presentation and appearance as to start out with two—or even three—strikes against them. Many show wildly mistaken assessments of the editorial needs of the publication to which they were sent. The market research simply was not done. Other poetical offerings are not timely, not accessible, not of the proper length....and so are simply not publishable.

Editors—as would anyone else—resent the time required to stuff such obviously unsuitable material into SASE's and mail them out again. (You didn't know they had to handle such menial chores themselves? Would that it were so. Unfortunately the shoe-string world of magazine publishing is not so well equipped with girl and guy Friday's as most writers imagine).

These are sad observations, but they are all too true. Yet, correctly submitting your poems to magazines is a simple, straightforward process. There are just a few rules to follow on the positive side and some pitfalls to avoid on the negative. That's not so much

Notes

"In literature as in love we are astonished at what is chosen by others."

Andre Maurois

Notes

to remember, but each item on the list is very important. Remember that you want the editor who evaluates your work to do so in the most favorable frame of mind possible. You may be new to the game. You may be totally inexperienced. You may be the rankest amateur. Fine. The important thing, though, is not to look like one.

Step One: Research the Market

When you truly research possible markets for your poems a strange thing happens. You become happily aware that there are far more outlets for your verse than you ever thought possible. If you are a careful writer and knowledgeable in your craft the odds of your finding a publisher are very much in your favor—when you utilize the methods suggested in this chapter.

When you prepare your submissions professionally and carry on an organized marketing campaign you will gradually begin to see your work in print, at first from time to time, them more and more frequently.

How do you go prospecting for poetry-publishing periodicals? Here are some ways to get started:

- You can begin with a reference book like *Poet's Market*, published by *Writer's Digest*. Frankly, though, this may not be your best source, and certainly it is very far from your only one. You will find listed in this directory many consumer and small press magazines that publish poetry. Select those that seem most likely to be interested in *your* work. When you have exhausted this source, though, you will have done nothing more than scratch the surface. Scores of regional and specialized publications will not be listed there.

- Next, go to your local library and browse through the periodical shelves. Pay special attention to regional magazines and house magazines. I am thinking, for instance, of a magazine like *Carolina Country*, which goes out monthly to several hundred thousand members of the North Carolina Rural Electrification Cooperative. Most of us would never think of this magazine, yet for the right poem of the right length on the right subject, it just might offer the opportunity you are looking for, even though it seldom publishes verse at all. A friend of mine recently wrote and illustrated a nifty little sixteen-page pamphlet which he titled *The Great Sweet*

Potato Cookbook. The recipes in it were entirely in rhyme. *Carolina Country,* with its strong emphasis on home and garden might have been perfect for these rhyming recipes. Placement there could easily have led to a continuing series ("The Rhyming Gourmet"?) and even a book. Anyone writing this kind of verse for a magazine of such powerful circulation will certainly build a broad base of faithful readers and the kind of strong name recognition on which successful careers are built.

- Search, too, for magazines published by private industries and for trade magazines. Topical poems on subjects of special interest to the editors of these magazines could very well find a home in their pages.

- Use your imagination as you study the offerings on the reading room shelf. Look for a slant, an approach as you pick up each and every publication. Ask yourself, "How can I fit in here." More often than you think an idea will pop into your mind. As is the way with such ideas, some of them will be good ones and will work for you.

- Don't neglect the newspapers. In addition to the daily papers there are in many communities smaller tabloids that cater to those interested in books, cultural events and the other arts. These may be just right for you. Even newsletters can be of interest to you.

- Research the periodical directories, such as *Gebbies All-in-One* and the *Gale Directory of Periodicals.* These valuable reference books contain listings for all but the most obscure publications, listed by type of editorial content.

- When you find a magazine that you think that you will want to submit to, write to request writer's guidelines. Don't forget to send SASE along with your request. These guidelines will probably be prepared primarily for writers of non-fiction articles, but the general information they contain about subject matter, editorial requirements and the general slant of the magazine will be quite valuable to you.

- Look through the magazines in doctor's offices, dentist's waiting rooms, the seatbacks of airplanes, the reception areas of businesses that you may enter during the week. Be

Notes

ever on the alert for possible outlets for your work. Carry a small notebook with you at all times to make note of the vital information (names, addresses) of magazines, newsletters and other publications that you find in such places.

• When in doubt, go ahead and add a publication to your list. As you begin to submit in a systematic way you will have ample opportunity to weed out the unsuitable names and add others that seem more likely to bring success. You are like a prospector looking for gold. You explore every possible source. Neglect one and you risk missing precisely the vein where the mother lode lies.

• The human mind being more like a sieve than a bucket, take careful notes on your market research. Note the name of the publication, the address, the editor's name (if there are several editors, choose the one that seems most appropriate), a brief description of the needs of the magazine and its editorial policies. Make note of the ways that you think your work can fit in with these policies. If you find any poems in the editions you look at, note the subject matter and *the average length*. Finally, make careful note of ideas for poems that occur to you in the course of your research and that you will write for the express purpose of filling a particular editorial need.

• When you have completed your basic market survey you should have scores—perhaps even hundreds—of names on your list. Some of these names will be known to very few poets—since most will not have done the spadework necessary to turn up the hot leads.

Create "Poem Packs"

With your prospect list in hand you now study the poems that you have on hand and that are ready to make the rounds of the editorial offices that you have targeted.

Let's say that you have forty top-notch, publishable pieces ready to mail out. Study these poems with an eye to creating what I will call "poem packs". These will be made up of verses with compatible themes and compatible lengths—thus appealing to similar markets. In addition, each poem included in the pack will have passed a significant number of the tests of publishability outlined

Notes

in Chapter 3. Since editors generally like to see more than one poem at a time, but grow restless at the prospect of reading more than four, I suggest that each of your poem packs contain at least two and no more than four pieces.

Now give each poem pack a number and carefully note the titles of the poems that it contains. You will want eventually to break them up into new combinations, and you want to know at a glance which editors have seen which of your poems.

The Key to Success: Organized Marketing

You have created these poem packs to facilitate your marketing effort and to help produce some early results. You are now ready to begin an intensive round of submissions, keeping all of your poems out for consideration all of the time. Since you have dozens of magazines on your prospect list it doesn't make sense to send everything out serially, waiting to hear from one publication before sending a batch out to another.

You will make up a "submissions record" form for each poem pack. I include one that works for me in this chapter. You are welcome simply to duplicate it and put it to your own use. I attribute my first sale to a major magazine (*Esquire*)to the rigorous, unrelenting use of this simple form. It enabled me to keep my submission alive until someone bought it, and that someone turned out to exceed my wildest expectation. Prior to that my queries spent more time in my desk drawer than they did in the editorial offices of magazines.

The same success can come to you, too, when you institute a *campaign of intensive, organized marketing.*

What we are talking about here is a well-planned effort whose goal is to get you published, as well and as often as possible. You simply can't keep up with the whirlwind activity of this method without this record-keeping. Neglect to use this form and you will forget what has been sent where. You will delay resubmitting poem packs that have been returned to you because you can't remember where you wanted to send them next.

Here's what you do:

* At the head of each form, fill in the number of the poem pack whose submissions it records.

* Then list, one after the other, the names and addresses of ten possible markets for these poems.

Notes

"Before people complain about the obscurity of modern poetry, they should first examine their consciences and ask themselves with how many people and on how many occasions they have genuinely and profoundly shared some experience with another...."

—*W.H. Auden*

- Send the pack to the first name on the list.

- If your work is accepted, great! If not, send it out again, *within twenty-four hours of its return.* Make this a hard and fast rule. *Never* keep a poem pack on hand more than a day. You can't sell what people can't see.

- Gradually, you'll begin to build a second, higher priority list, made up of the names of editors who either buy your work, express an interest in your work even though they don't buy, or include an encouraging, hand-written notation of some kind on their rejection slip. You will want to send something to those on this priority list at least once a month until you've got nothing more to send.

The Professional Submission

The submission itself is quite simple to prepare. Yet, simple as it is not only some, but *most*, of the poets who have sent their work in to me over the years have failed to follow the basic rules of literary etiquette that successful writers all observe. The goal is to make your poems easy to handle, easy to read and easy to think about. Here are the rules of he game:

- Each poem will be typed, double-spaced, on a sheet of good quality white bond.

- In the upper left hand corner you will write your name and address.

- In the upper right hand corner write the number of lines in your poem and the rights you offer for sale. Most editors are quite content with the basic first serial rights offer.

- Many of your poems will be complete on one page. In the event that a poem requires two or more pages be certain that the pages are numbered sequentially and that your name and the rights information appear on each page. Most word processing programs can handle this "header" information for you and save you the burden of having to retype it quite so often.

- Include a cover letter, personally addressed to the ap-

Notes

Notes

propriate editor. If you don't know the editor's name and if you have not been able to find it on the masthead, call the magazine and ask for it. Avoid a "Dear Editor" letter. Your one-page cover letter very succinctly (1) offers the poems for consideration; (2) gives some subtle (I emphasize *subtle*) indication that you are familiar with the editor's publication and its needs; and (3) briefly mentions your best credentials ("My poems have appeared in..."), if any. You should omit this section rather than list the time you had a quatrain appear in the high school newspaper or on your family Christmas card. This cover letter, like the poems themselves, is cleanly typed on good white bond.

- Include a self-addressed, stamped envelope.

- This last recommendation is a personal preference. I do it with my own work, even though it is a bit more expensive. I do not fold my submissions for mailing in a standard, number 10 envelope. I mail them flat in a large, white catalogue envelope. These unfolded submissions, even when just a few pages long, are easier to handle and easier to read. More than any other kind of writing, poems have a visual impact on the reader. It is good to see them entire, on a flat, unfolded piece of paper. However, this procedure is certainly optional, and I leave you to make up your own mind which is better for you.

The Dirty Dozen: Twelve Beginner's Mistakes You Must Avoid

Newcomers to the ranks of professional writing stamp themselves as beginners in characteristic ways. Carefully avoiding these errors will put you in a much stronger marketing position.

- Do not include a note telling how much your family and friends think of your talent and how they encouraged you to send these poems in.

- Do not inform the editor that you are sure that these poems are "just what his readers have been waiting for" and that your "feel certain that they will love them". Leave such judgments up to the editor.

- Do not include notice of copyright on your poems. Under the terms of the current copyright act your work is protected anyway. Notice of copyright on a submission suggests legal problems and hints that you may be difficult to deal with. Your editor may want to buy first serial rights, all rights or no rights. Time enough to worry about copyright after the deal is done.

- Do not submit poems in longhand. No one will take time to decipher them.

- Don't specify what payment you wish to receive. This is for later. When an editor accepts your work he will tell you what his rates are. At that time you can accept or reject them, or perhaps negotiate an adjustment. In poetry, it's a buyer's market.

- Do not include photos or drawings to illustrate your poems, no matter how perfect you think you child's, your spouse's or your lover's effort is. Art is handled by a magazine's designers. Writer-furnished art is seldom required. If you have something that is truly outstanding you might mention it in your cover letter. If the editor responds and asks to see it you can send it along.

- Don't neglect to send SASE.

- Don't give an editor a deadline for replying. Write a follow-up letter if there is a long delay in giving you a decision. If there is still no response send your poem pack out to the next name on the list.

- Don't submit your work on fancy, colored paper.

- Don't submit your work on paper of non-standard size. Stick to eight-and-a-half by eleven.

- Don't send out soiled or shopworn material. It is too easy these days to print out fresh copies on your word processor.

A simple marketing method for getting your poetry into magazines? You bet. But put it into action in the service of your own work and I will virtually guarantee you that if your poetry has any merit at all it will find its way into print.

Notes

Chapter 5

How to Find a Publisher for Your Book of Poetry

Imagine this. You hold a book in your hands. Opening the book you see that the title page announces a collection of poems. In the place where the author's name appears, you read your own name. And leafing through the volume you see your own poems.

A dream? Perhaps, but one that can come true far more easily than you may think. In fact, it is a dream that is becoming more easily realized every day. You *can* interest a small publisher in your book if you have four things:

- A good collection of poems sufficient to make a small book, say three dozen or more, depending on length. It is a plus if some of these have previously appeared in magazines, journals or other periodicals, thus creating the beginning of a positive track record for you and your work.

- A willingness (which you clearly communicate to your publisher) to assume the responsibility for self-promotion and for publicizing and selling your book. Give details of what you plan. This is nowhere near as hard as it seems. A

"...What is known as success assumes nearly as many aliases as there are those who seek it. Like love, it can come to commoners as well as courtiers. Like virtue, it is its own reward. Like the Holy Grail, it seldom appears to those who don't pursue it."

—Stephen Birmingham

self-promotion starter kit is given below. It is easy to use and *it works*. Remember, if you want to be successful, it is not enough to *be* a poet. You have to see to it that potential readers *know* that you are a poet.

- The desire, energy and know-how to make it happen. You supply the poems, the desire and the energy. In the pages which follow I will supply the know-how.

- A willingness to assume some or all of the out-of-pocket expenses for publishing your book, whether from a grant, an institution (the college or school you work for, for instance) or your own bank account. As I have said many times in this book it is not only permissible but usually *expected* that poets will participate in the publication of their work.

The Changing World of Publishing

Publishing today is a highly diversified enterprise. It is no longer centralized in the metropolitan areas of New York and Boston, though this was the case just a few years ago. The technological revolution known as desktop publishing, along with the development of very affordable short-run offset printing techniques, has made it possible for many small—even minuscule—publishing companies to rise and flourish at viable levels of activity.

More Publishers Than You Think

There are likely to be more book publishers out there than you can possibly imagine. I recently attempted to contact and list every publishing company in my home state of North Carolina. I thought it would be easy, a matter of a couple of days research. I was very, very mistaken. I knew the largest regional houses, of course—firms like John F. Blair, the University of North Carolina Press and Algonquin Books. But there were dozens of others—Briarpatch Press, Mud Puppy Press, Ventana Books, North Carolina Wesleyan Press, Scots Plaid Press, St. Andrews College Press and many others, including my own Venture Press. I had published books and magazines in North Carolina for years and I was discovering excellent small presses that I had never heard of before. I have been at it a month now, and new names are added to my list almost daily. You will doubtlessly encounter much the same situation in

Notes

your part of the country.

Many of these presses are little known to the general public or even to writers. Few of them will be listed in directories such as *Writer's Market* or even *Literary Market Place*. Yet they are there, and they may very well be interested in publishing your book.

You will need names and addresses of these editor/publishers in order to approach them. How do you get the information you need? In several ways:

- Visit bookstores that specialize in literary and small press books. You will usually find these in university towns and seldom elsewhere. Browse the poetry sections. Collect names and addresses of publishers from the title pages of books that interest you.

- Join your state or local poetry society and network with the other members.

- Join writer's clubs and writer's support groups on the local and state level, again networking with other members.

- Contact book review editors of major newspapers in your state. They can often help. A telephone call will work best, since they will not usually have time to answer mail inquiries.

- Check the catalogue in the library of your state university. At the University of North Carolina at Chapel Hill, for instance, there is a North Carolina Collection with its own curator. The collection tries hard to include a copy of every book published in North Carolina or written by North Carolinians.

Your state will have such a collection, too. If the curator is a gregarious sort, he or she may be willing to talk to you personally, sharing whatever information they have. Rarely, however, will the curator have all the facts you need. You will need to search through the card catalogue.

Today you can often access the library's catalogue by computer, often from your own home, making your task much easier and far less time consuming. Again, you will note names and addresses of author/publishers. If this is not available, get the names of the authors and contact them directly.

Notes

Submitting Your Poems

Your marketing effort begins when you approach the prospective publisher. You will send in your poems in the same clean, professional format described in the preceding chapter. You are merely sending more of them. You will make your publisher aware of any credentials and credits that you have accumulated. Just make sure that the credits you enumerate are solid ones. If you have never been published before your task is more difficult.

You've got to come across to your publisher as not only talented and deserving but as energetic and promotion-prone as well. Of course, there is always the case of the poet whose first effort is a masterstroke of pure genius. If you are one of these rare birds, congratulations! But even in this case it is you, as poet, who have to take the initiative to see that your work is published. Nothing happens of and by itself. It is you who make it happen.

The Publisher's Mindset

You will be aware of the publisher's mindset that we discussed earlier. Though most publishers understand and accept the fact that no one is likely to make much money on a book of poems, he will certainly want to avoid a loss.

To reassure the publisher that his investment of time and money in your work is safe, you will want to furnish him with the following items, information and assurances:

- The poems themselves, very neatly typed and prepared according to the most professional standards. Your submission will be crisp and clean, not smudged and dog-eared. There will be no strikeovers or hand-written corrections. To submit your poems in this way conveys to the editor the impression that he holds in his hands the work of a professional, someone who can be relied on to meet commitments and follow through on promises. Not to do so will brand you as an amateur unwilling to take the time to see that his own work is carefully prepared and presented. Such an impression is not reassuring to the editor.

- If any of your poems have been published in magazines, journals or other periodicals, provide a neatly typed list of these credits on your fact sheet.

Notes

- Provide tear sheets of any reviews, profiles or other write-ups that will help establish you as a poet with marketable public visibility.

- If you have published a book of poetry in the past that sold well (300 to 500 copies in a reasonably short period of time), then the publisher whom you are now approaching should be made aware of that success. Such facts will make it easier for him to believe that the same thing can be done again. How did you promote the book? Who bought it? For how much? Give all the details.

- Tell the publisher how you propose to help market your book once it is published. Where will you have opportunities to do readings. How often? The fact is that books of poetry are seldom bought in bookstores. They are almost always bought at readings, lectures, school appearances and similar events. The publisher knows that no amount of effort on his part will sell your book. It is the poet alone who can do this. Let him know—in as much detail as possible—that you are ready, willing and able to do your part.

- Make it clear that, if need be, you can help with the costs of publication. I keep coming back to this fact because it is important. It is not unusual today for publishers to ask poets to assist in footing the bill for publication. This request rests on solid economic grounds. Even if an edition of 300 sells out the publisher, after paying royalties, costs of production, office overhead and other associated costs, will not show a profit sufficient to pay for his time. You can call your expenditure a subsidy, an investment or come up with any other label you wish. Whatever you call it, this kind of arrangement is perfectly acceptable today, so long as the publisher is one of reputation and not a mere vanity profiteer.

Such financial arrangements are fast becoming the rule rather that the exception. As Judson Jerome pointed out in his popular *Writer's Digest* column, a book of verse is published *for* the poet. It is not a part of the publisher's normal, income-producing work. Why should the poet, Jerome asked, *not* pay part of the costs?

This can be a very professional and thoroughly workable cooperative effort. Such a system has, indeed, been the norm for many years in the field of academic publishing. It is rare to get a book published by any but the most affluent univer-

---

Notes

"Unless you're a closet Shakespeare, your words will never fall onto the paper just right on your first try. There are too many words in the language, too many shades of meaning, too many opportunities to be just a bit more precise or effective. Your first try can never be just retyped and shipped off to a waiting editor. Would-be writers who make that mistake become has-beens before they ever break into the field."

—*Franklynn Peterson and Judi Kesselman-Turkel, in* The Magazine Writer's Handbook. Dood, Mead & Co., 1987.

Notes

sity presses these days without coming up with a sizable contribution to the cost of publication. Sometimes the subsidies come in the form of grants from local, state or national foundations or arts organizations. Sometimes the author's home university or college will provide the necessary funds. Sometimes it is the author himself who foots the bill.

Is this "vanity publishing". Absolutely not. The so-called vanity presses of the "New York Publisher Seeks Books" variety will publish virtually anything that is submitted to them. Their sole motive is the profit motive. To indulge it they charge the author an arm and a leg.

The presses we are talking about do not work this way. Their chief motive in publishing poetry is to publish good poetry. They merely want to avoid a negative balance sheet and so stay in business. Money may talk, but among the reputable presses it will get you only so far. You could not buy your way on to the University of North Carolina Press list for any sum of money. Only the highest quality will get you there. Books are read carefully and fastidiously evaluated. Only those found to be worthy are accepted. Then and only then does the question of money arise—at which point the university presses and other independent publishers will sometimes explore the possibility of an author-generated subsidy.

You, as a poet, will be known to some extent by the company you keep. That company is not very illustrious with the vanity presses. Remember, they will publish anything that comes along so long as the author has the big bucks to pay them all costs as well as a handsome, up-front profit. Reviewers, who know all this, will not usually take the trouble even to browse through a book which bears the imprint of the vanity presses on its title page.

They will, however, read the books published by even the smallest independent publishers, especially those which have built a reputation for quality. With the small publishers you can be in exemplary company indeed. If such a publisher asks you to contribute financially to the publication of your book do not be insulted. Merely check the titles and quality of the other books that his company has in print. If these are books of excellence, then you can feel safe in entrusting your work into his hands as well.

Notes

Chapter 6

The Unabashed Poet's Guide to Publicity and Self-Promotion

Your poems and books of poems will sell if you make them sell. I don't mean that you have to hawk them like the guy pushing overpriced Polish sausage at the state fair, though that beats not selling them at all. You can bring your book to market with professionalism and dignity. But you must also do it as energetically and as aggressively as your personality will permit.

You will have to blow your own horn a bit. Sometimes you can do this behind the scenes by making it possible and very easy for other people to do the blowing for you. News releases, when carefully written, will appear in the pages of local and regional newspapers, so long as you do the work of writing them and sending them out. A reviewer may blow your horn for you so long as you put the horn (your book) in his hands in the first place. Autograph parties and readings will be rousing successes so long as you carefully schedule, organize and stage them.

You must understand and accept the fact that if you want to be known as a poet you will have to take steps to make yourself known as a poet. This chapter tells you how.

You must not underrate the importance of following this prescription for building literary success through building a

"(There has been) a very peculiar bias...that is only now beginning to erode. This is the sense that publishing a book is an act somehow outside the main avenues of commerce; that people who deal with ideas should not sully themselves with such crass concerns as salesmanship, advertising, market share—with finding, in fact, an audience for what the writer...has so laboriously created."

—Robert A. Carter, in **Trade Book Marketing**

41

literary reputation. The personal, professional and even financial rewards which will come to the writer who sees to his own welfare are very substantial indeed. While there are exceptions to every generalization, you can accept it as 99.99% true that there are no reputations in any field that are not *made* reputations. Don't count on the good fairy to do what you are unwilling to do for yourself. The good fairy is a notorious phony and will seldom take time to fulfill your basic needs, much less your fondest expectations.

As a poet you and you alone are the chief marketer of your wares as well as your reputation. A poet I know recently sold 100 of his books just after they come off the press. The book had a regional theme, and he sold this large batch to the County Development Commission, which uses them to highlight cultural activities in the area when they make their pitch to top industrial client. The money from this one sale came close to paying the out-of-pocket printing costs.

The Development Commission did not come to him. He went to them. Had he waited, alone, in his study for the hordes to come knocking at his door and demanding his product, no sale would even have been made. He did not wait. He acted on his idea. He made it happen.

This same poet scheduled a series of readings (see the chapter "How to Give a Reading", below) at which he sold even more books. He has entered his book in state competitions, been reviewed in top newspapers, used his book to land jobs teaching creative writing at community colleges. You can do the same things.

Notice carefully that I use the active voice. He did these things. They were not done to him or for him. Contrary to what our mothers may have told us, the world does not care a fig whether we succeed in our endeavors or not. Nature could care less whether we make it as published poets. The atmospheric pressure at sea level and the rate of acceleration due to gravity are totally indifferent to our fate. No, there's nothing out there that is going to do it for us. We succeed only when we harness our own brains, energies and talents and do the things we have to do to succeed.

Here's how to get started.

Prepare a Media Kit

These used to be called press kits, as though television didn't exist, but no more. The media kit is your most important informa-

Notes

tion packet, and it is designed to make the work of those from whom you hope to get coverage that much easier.

Each item in it will have multiple uses. Sometimes you will send the complete kit. Sometimes you will send the news release or some other item alone.

A complete media kit will contain the following items:

- A fact sheet on yourself as author. This fact sheet will include a short bio of you, a listing of your credits, short excerpts from favorable reviews or interviews, a statement of your goals and motivations as a writer, quotable quotes, etc. Keep it in easily utilized, outline form so that a feature writer or reviewer can easily find and excerpt materials that are needed for a write-up.

- In preparing this fact sheet, as in preparing all the other marketing materials in your repertoire, bear in mind that reporters—whether print or electronic—will not have time to research an article on you and your work. You have to do this for them. When your fact sheet is well done and easily utilized you take a giant step toward getting the kind of publicity you need.

- The fact sheet can also be used as a background piece to include in your poetry submissions to magazines and to publishers. It can be given to program chairmen who have to introduce you to audiences before whom you are scheduled to appear. You can have it blown up to poster size and use it as a prop at readings, autograph parties and other occasions.

- Your media kit will also include a fact sheet on your book. What press published it? How many pages? What about special themes? What about quotes to illustrate these themes? How can the book be obtained? At what price? Your book fact sheet may well include an item or two that also appears on your personal fact sheet. Don't worry about necessary duplication but don't repeat materials needlessly.

- Clips of any pre-publication or other reviews (or interviews) that you may have had. You will photocopy these and keep them readily available.

- Copies of any other articles that may have been written

"You won't get far by . . . being timid and underestimating your abilities or worth. I meet students and new writers who say: 'I'd write a story for nothing in order to get into print!' That, and any notion remotely akin to it, is the attitude of an amateur, and editors, though often willing to gamble on a new writer, are never drawn to amateurism. The professional writer is not one to stand around humbly, like a beggar at the backdoor. He tries to offer something good, and in a manner that suggests self-confidence, and self-esteem."
—Hayes Jacobs, in
Writing and Selling
Non-Fiction

about you.

- A brief news release of one full page or less. While a news release is a short, straightforward story telling that you wrote your book and that it was published, always lead with the strongest reader-pulling fact about the book you can come up with.

- A complete feature article of 500 to 700 words, with photographs. This piece is an in-depth personality profile of you and your work. Will the article be used? Sometimes it will and sometimes it won't. It all depends on the space availability and intrinsic interest of your article. One thing, though, is certain. It will certainly not be used if you do not write it. Most newspapers are understaffed and do not have a regular book review editor. Some writers will use your article as a guide. Some—especially weeklies, which will be happy to have a free feature—will print it just as you provide it. Always manage to tell readers how and where they can buy your book. Include a mention for instance, like "*My Book of Poems* was published by Muse Books of Tupelo, Mississippi." Also include a mention of the retail price.

    Is there anything wrong with your writing articles about yourself? Absolutely not. That's the way it's done.

- Include a glossy, black and white photograph of yourself. Some kind of action shot in a natural surrounding will get a better play than a simple mug shot since it will have greater reader interest. If you are writing a poem about your conquest of Mt. Everest the photograph ought to show you on the summit.

Send Out Review Copies

Don't be stingy with review copies. Don't waste them, of course, but do send one to every publication that you feel might review your book. The cost of sending these copies will be one of the best investments you will make.

Send your media kit along with your book to weekly newspapers and smaller dailies. For major dailies with a regular book reviewer, send a book along with a picture and your fact sheet.

There may be periodicals and radio and TV stations that you

Notes

truly feel are marginal. In these cases you may not want to send a copy of your book. Send instead a cover letter, a personal fact sheet, and a reply card for use in requesting a review copy. When a card from such a mailing comes in, send along your book personally addressed to the individual who requested the review copy. Include your fact sheets, again, with the book. The likelihood that they will have been misplaced in the interim is great. You may also elect to send your complete media kit with the review copy.

Important: Everything that you send out should be on the publishing company letterhead. The review package should come from the publisher (that's you as publisher or someone else as publisher) rather than from you personally.

The exception to this rule comes when you know the reviewer personally or when you have personal contacts on your local newspaper. In such cases, if possible, you can hand deliver the package or arrange a lunch date at which you can better pitch your product.

If you do an autograph signing or is there is some celebration of the publication of your book, a good black-and-white photograph showing you at the occasion could make it into print when you live in a relatively small town. Such a photograph is not likely to get much attention on its own in a major metropolitan area.

Your local library will have a reference book containing lists of contact persons and addresses of the media, large and small, in your state. Always address your review material to an individual, by name, whenever possible.

Lesser, but Powerful Promotional Publications

Do not overlook association newsletters, organizational magazines and other lesser publications. These can be a great help in creating the kind of public recognition that you are after.

If there are other tie-ins, be sure to exploit them. If your poetry commemorates some historical occasion, and if you are a member of the DAR, for instance, send a package to the organization's magazine or newsletter editor. If you are a member of the American Legion and your poetry has a patriotic theme, send a copy to the American Legion Magazine. You won't hit many of the national publications at the right time, and you will have to understand that the competition for limited space is fierce. But take advantage of every possibility. You will not get your message into print every time you attempt to do so, but when you do succeed the results can be very important to you.

Notes

You can ask to have a copy of any review sent to you, but normally this is not done. You will not know of reviews in papers you don't regularly read until some acquaintance tells you, casually, "Hey, I read that article about your book in the paper last week."

Bombard the World with News Releases

You will not want to send you complete media kit to everyone. It is too expensive. But you should send a news release to every possible source of publicity.

The news release (see sample) will tell the person who reads it where he or she can get more information and a review copy. If any one requests that you send them this additional material you can then send the complete kit.

Do news releases work? You bet they do. Some time back I organized a small publishing company to bring out a commercial magazine. Everything worked fine, except for one thing. Since I was new in business the printer wanted to be paid in advance. Yet, I could not collect from my advertisers until I had the published magazine in hand. Where was I going to get the $20,000 I needed to pay the printer with?

I went to the banks. They liked what I was doing but politely pointed out that I had no track record. I thought about this response and realized that these bankers had just never heard of me or my company before. I set about to remedy that. I sent small news releases out weekly. My company was bringing out this new magazine or that, expanding its operations into this area or that, hiring this person or that as vice-president for sales (vice-presidents get into print more easily than sales managers) and every other positive thing that could possibly be imagined. I concluded each short release with a paragraph about my position as president and my own credentials.

After three months I approached a new bank. "Yes," the banker said, "I have heard of you and your company. You're doing quite well. How can I help?" And in short order I had the line of credit I needed. I was the same. My company was the same. I had merely increased my positive public visibility through the effective use of news releases.

A news release is not a feature story. It tells, in the terse style of straight news stories, the facts of your book and its publication. The best releases will be one page in length. This length is manageable and fits easily into filler space in newspapers. In no case should your release run more than a page and a half unless there

They say that every good news story should tell the basic facts: who, what, where, when, how. This is certainly true, but to the list you must add one more item: So what? If you want your news story to be picked up by the majority of the papers you send it to, get to the so what? part of it in the lead sentence. Give the reader, up front, a good reason to continue through the article and the editor, therefore, a very good reason for publishing it.

is something far more newsworthy involved than the mere fact that you have written and published a book.

The shorter and more concise the news release the more likely it is to be picked up by newspapers.

Always write your release in newspaper style. No one will have time to rewrite it, and it will be discarded. If you do not feel that you can copy the style of newspapers you can get a journalist to write one for you. A one-page release will cost about $50, but it may be worth it if this is the only way you can get it done. Perhaps through your writer's club you will know of a newspaper person who will do it for you without a fee. It really takes very little time when you know the formula.

News releases must fit available space. This means that editors often lop off a final paragraph or two when they put your release in place. Since you know that this often happens you will get all essential information in the first few paragraphs. The closing portion, while containing readable information, will be expendable. The release will stand alone with or without them.

A Release for Every Occasion

When should you send out news releases? There are more occasions than you might imagine. Remember that your goal is not only to sell a particular book but to build your reputation as a poet and literary figure of importance.

Here are some typical occasions that merit news releases:

• You publish a poem in a journal or magazine of note.

• You publish a book. Send a separate release on acceptance and another on publication.

• You are honored at an autograph party.

• You give a talk to a club.

• You give a reading.

• You are elected to an office in an arts organization.

• You start your own publishing company.

Notes

How to Get on Television

There are several steps to getting on television. You can succeed, but you may have to throw out several lines to catch a single fish.

Your first move is to send out a television news release. This varies somewhat from from a print media news release, but it conveys the same basic information.

- Include a routing box on your television news release as follows:

> Routing:
> ❑ News Director
> ❑ Lifestyle
> ❑ Talkshow host

- You will want to double and triple up on your television contacts. Your news release should be beefed up with your complete media kit, sent to talk show hosts by name, and by personal telephone calls to the same individuals.

- Send out "available for interview" sheets to talk show hosts. These sheets are designed to tell them, at a glance, why you will be a good interview. This is worth some effort, as it is good business to be seen on local and regional talk shows. These shows are constantly on the lookout for anybody doing anything interesting, and you, as a published poet, can fill that bill, so long as you let them know just *why* what you have to say will be interesting. This sheet will include your photo in the upper right hand corner, your brief bio, a section telling what your book is about and, most important, a section suggesting strong viewer-pulling topics, i.e., "How to unlock the creative force within."

- Give them the double whammy. Call them directly *and* send them an available for interview sheet.

- A tip: no-shows are a constant problem on local talk shows. When you speak to the talk show host let them know that you are available on short notice and can fill in for last-minute cancellations—a sure way to get your good-looking profile on camera in short order.

Notes

How to Prepare for a Television Interview

If you will follow through on these suggestions you are certainly going to get on the air. The next step is to prepare carefully for your interview. These do not last long: five minutes is the usual, sometimes stretching to ten if commercial time is not filled or if a later guest fails to show up. What will you talk about? Think carefully about this and develop some material that will be as broadly interesting as you can make it.

- Type five or six of the most interesting and leading questions you can think of on an index card. Give this card to the person who is going to interview you. This person will seldom have read your book and will be grateful for your help in making the interview go well.

- Try to come up with questions that will capture the attention of your viewers. "They say that everybody has a book or a poem inside them just waiting to get out. How do you open the creative doors?", and "What advice do you have for aspiring poets" might be two good ones.

- You might also plant a question about a specific poem that you think will be of interest to your viewers. You will doubtless come up with some great ideas that grow out of your own work and interests.

- Remember that you are the expert. Project an air of confidence and authority. Remember my advice (below) on self-deprecation. There is certainly no place for it on television. Too much untimely modesty can make for a poor interview.

- Always let your viewers know what your book title is and what it is about. Let them know where it can be bought. When you go on the air make arrangements for a local bookstore to have some copies on hand. Some listeners will undoubtedly go out and buy a copy.

- Television is a visual medium. Take care with your appearance. Study the show that you are going on. Do the guests sit in chairs? Behind desks? Practice your posture and bearing.

- Bring along an art board that displays the cover of your book

Notes

"A few weeks from now I will publish a collection of poetry by a very gifted young writer. Since he is personable and will do effective — and numerous—public readings I expect to sell out the first printing of 500 copies by the end of the year. If I do the book will be considered profitable. The author will have his royalties and I will have paid my suppliers and have a small sum left over to help publish someone else's collection of verse next year."

—Thomas A. Williams,
How to Make $100,000
a Year in Desktop
Publishing.

or one or two of your poems neatly spray-mounted in place and perhaps bordered. Give this to the director of the show beforehand. They may ask the host to hold up a copy, but they may also use your art board as a lead-in or lead-out.

- Do not neglect radio talk shows. These shows have a tremendous popularity today. I never fail to get calls and inquiries whenever I appear on one of them. Often you will have as much as thirty minutes of time to talk about your work, the writing life, etc.

- After your appearance the station phones will ring. Many listeners and viewers will have missed the part where you tell them how to get hold of your book. Leave a "for further information" card with the show's host and with the station's switchboard operator. On the card will be your name and address, the title of your book, and details on how and where to buy a copy of it. Alert bookstores to the possible increased demand.

Announce Your Book to Relatives, Friends and Acquaintances

When marketing a book of poetry every sale counts. Three to five hundred transactions will exhaust the entire first edition.

It does not take too many of them, therefore, to make your book a rousing success.

One often overlooked market is that of family and friends. Utilize your Christmas card list, for instance, or your child's wedding announcement list. Under the publisher's name (even if your are the publisher) send an announcement of publication in a social invitation size envelope. The card inside will bear the message that "Orpheus Publications has the honor to announce the publication of (your title) by (your name)". Then give the date of publication. In the same envelope is another card with the publisher's address on one side and a place for a stamp. On the other side is an order blank. Be sure to state that the copies sent in response to the order will be copies of the first edition and that they will be signed by the author. Also include the price, or course. It usually generates additional sales to provide space for the names and addresses of those to whom gift copies might can be sent, should the buyer wish to order them. Since you do not want to be in the business of billing your friends for books they have bought, indicate that a check

Notes

for the purchase (with $1 additional for postage) should be included with the reply card.

You may wish to delay sending this announcement for friends whom you expect to invite to your first big marketing gala, your publication autograph party.

Notes

(A news release in the form of a feature story might begin like this. It would be sent to a newspaper -- especially smaller papers or weeklies -- along with an interesting photo of the author. Always include two or three poems with permission to reprint, and include quotes from poems in the text of the review itself. Don't forget to include ordering info for those who would like to obtain a copy.)

Venture Press
104 South Respess Street
Washington, NC 27889
(919) 975-2066

For further information:
Thomas A. Williams, Ph.D.
Publisher
(919) 975-2066

FOR IMMEDIATE RELEASE

New Book Captures People, Places and Spirit
of Historic Washington

"When I first came to the town of Washington, I just knew I had to write about it", says poet Jane Doe of her new book, Visions of Washington. "It all fascinated me -- the river and the marshes, the fishermen in the early morning fog, the rich heritage and history, and especially the people. There is a sense of place here, of roots, that seems so often to be missing these days. I found them all here in this little seacoast town."

Doe's book, her third, was published early this month by Venture Press. "We believe it is one of the best we have done in some time," says publisher Tom Williams. "Visions of Washington will be a serious contender for the J.J. Jones Medal, awarded by the Literary Society to the best book of poetry by a North Carolinian."

Many of Vision's poems profile individuals Doe came to know and admire during her year-long stay. Here, for instance, is Calvin Cullers, tending his nets in the dim light of a river dawn:

(and the article continues with quotes and commentary)

John Doe
111 South Muse Place
Artsville, NC   12345

For further information:
(919) 999-4321

FOR IMMEDIATE RELEASE

Artsville Poet Honored

Artsville poet John Doe has been named winner of the North Carolina Society of Poetry award for best poem on a North Carolina theme for 1991.

In making the award, Marvin Major, President of the Society, singled out Doe's "deep understanding of the values that we all cherish: home, family and community."

Doe's verse has previously appeared in national and regional publications. He is also author of the recently published book, <u>Scenes</u> <u>of</u> <u>the</u> <u>Outer</u> <u>Banks</u>. Doe is a member of the Artsville Council for the Arts, and Secretary of the creative writing division of the North Carolina Literature Coalition.

End.

Note to the editor: The enclosed poem may be reproduced "by permission of John Doe. Copyright by John Doe, 1991." Review copies of <u>Scenes</u> <u>of</u> <u>the</u> <u>Outer</u> <u>Banks</u> may be obtained by calling the telephone number at the top of this release. John Doe is available for interview on topics of literary and artistic interest to the community.

John Doe
111 South Muse Place
Artsville, NC 12345

For further information:
(919) 999-4321

FOR IMMEDIATE RELEASE

───

Local Writer Will Appear

Artsville poet John Doe will appear on the WWWW-TV show, "The State of the Arts", this Sunday afternoon at 3:30. The show is hosted by Magnus Magnison, and features people and personalities in the Tri-City arts community.

Doe's recent book, <u>Scenes of the Outer Banks</u> (Venture Press, 1991), has been widely and positively reviewed. Doe also is the recipient of this year's North Carolina Poetry Society award for best poem on a North Carolina theme.

Doe is a member of the Artsville Council on the Arts, and Secretary of the North Carolina Coalition for Literature. He is currently a consultant in creative writing to the Artsville School System.

Doe is currently at work on a new book, <u>Southern Porches</u>, which will be published next year.

End.

Note to the editor: The enclosed poem may be reproduced "by permission of John Doe. Copyright by John Doe, 1991." Review copies of <u>Scenes of the Outer Banks</u> may be obtained by calling the telephone number at the top of this release. John Doe is available for interview on topics of literary and artistic interest to the community.

(Your "Available for Interview" form will give some hard information and tell why you will be an interesting and entertaining guest. It will include your photograph, credentials, and a listing of topics you are prepared to talk about, expressed in the strongest, most viewer-centered language you can come up with. Here, in abbreviated form, is an Available for Interview form that I might invent for this book on publishing poetry. My thanks to writer Peggy Glenn, whose book Publicity for Books and Authors I have quoted elsewhere, for suggesting this marketing idea.)

AVAILABLE FOR INTERVIEW

Tom Williams, Ph.D., noted author, editor and publisher. Author of the best-selling book, How to Publish Your Poetry: The First Ever Marketing Manual and Success Guide for Poets. Williams is the author of other books such as Tales of the Tobacco Country, a collection of history and folklore, How to Make $100,000 a Year in Desktop Publishing, and Breaking Free: How to Win Financial Freedom Through Your Home-based Business.

YOUR PHOTO HERE

He is President of Venture Press, a book publishing company based in Washington, NC, and former editor and publisher of Tar Heel: The Magazine of North Carolina.

On your show, Dr. Williams will talk about such topics as:

■ How to unlock the hidden wells or creativity within. Is there a book or a poem inside you? Now you can write it and even publish it! Dr. Williams tells how.

■ How to find hundreds of little-known magazines that will publish your poems.

■ How you can publish and sell a book of your own poems.

The interview is fun and stimulating. Thousands of everyday people are starved for creative expression, and Dr. Williams' ideas and encouragement tell them how to release this creative power in their own lives.

I will be available in your area on: _____

I will be available to substitute on short notice:_____Yes _____No

CONTACT:

Dr. Tom Williams, 104 South Respess Street, Washington, NC 27889
(919) 975-2066

Notes

One thing you want to be very careful to do is to note the name and address of every person who buys your book or comes to a reading. You can do this very easily and naturally by asking for name and address at the time of the purchase or by asking attendees at a reading to fill out an "information sheet." This list, added to the one you used to send out invitations to your autograph party constitutes your own mailing list of persons interested in you and your books. It will grow and grow as you appear more and more frequently in public. Whenever you bring out a new book you will send a pre-publication notice and special offer on an autographed first edition to those whose names are on your list. You will also use it to recruit people for workshops or seminars that you may give or any consulting services that you may, in time, wish to offer to less experienced, less market-wise poets.

Chapter 7

Your Unabashed Autograph Party Or, The Joys of Signing and Selling

Your book is out. News releases have generated stories in your local newspaper and you have appeared in an interview slot on that local morning talk show. The time is ripe for a publication and autograph party—the unabashed poet's first major marketing event or events, since there is no law that says that you can only have one of them.

The autograph party will follow very shortly after publication. And, make no mistake about it, it is wholly a marketing occasion. I don't mean that you can't enjoy yourself, of course. On the contrary, it's quite pleasant to be the center of all that attention.

Nevertheless, the autograph party is not something that someone does to you and for you while you linger humbly in the background until the time comes to have the roses thrown your way. No, a successful autograph party is very carefully planned and orchestrated to achieve two important goals:

- To focus attention on you and your work and thus enhance your reputation and public visibility. The more powerfully and professionally this is done the better you will be for it.

• To sell enough of your books to recoup the up-front publication costs.

To accomplish these goals your autograph party must be as rigidly controlled an event as any you have ever been associated with. There is no room for the amateurish or the tentative.

You Can't Leave It Up to Someone Else

The marketing of an artistic reputation or product (your book) requires all the basic know-how that you have been absorbing from this book. It is unlikely that even the closest of friends will possess the necessary skills to stage an effective marketing event.

This means that no matter who serves as the official host or hostess—whether an individual or a group—you will have to take charge of the arrangements and see that it is all done right. The autograph party has to be scheduled at the right time, the right people have to be invited, the evening planned so as to reach a climax when you want it to, and the purchase of your books made to seem as natural and inevitable as breathing.

You will begin to make plans for your autograph party even before the initial publication publicity appears. Nor is it necessary that you have only one of them. You may be able to arrange several in a larger town. But the first of them will be the major one, the one that serves as a kick-off celebration for your new life as a published poet.

Who Will Sponsor Your Party

Your publication/autograph party may be hosted by an individual or by a group. It may be given by:

a. An arts council
b. A poetry society
c. A writer's club
d. A friend
e. Your publisher, as main sponsor or, better, as co-sponsor

When someone expresses an interest in giving an autograph party for you ask yourself if this person is capable of putting together the event with your help (make sure that they will *accept* your help). Do they have the space? Do they have the social clout? If an organization, does it have an active membership? Are they

Notes

willing, with your help, to send out large numbers of invitations? Can they schedule the autograph party at a time of day most conducive to the best attendance?

You should get positive answers to most of these questions, if possible. If your sponsor does not check out against these success criteria, go ahead, but be prepared to do even more of the work yourself.

The Guest List

You will want to send invitations to the most extensive guest list possible. To do this do not hesitate to offer to help with the costs of printing invitations or postage, if you believe that this will facilitate things.

Your host (or host organization) will undoubtedly rely on you to provide names and addresses of those whom you wish to invite. You should include the following:

- Your own family, friends and acquaintances. These are essentially people who, though they may not be interested in poetry, are surely interested in you and who will come to be a part of the celebration.

- Members of the local arts council.

- Members of any local writers clubs to which you belong.

- Media representatives and contacts.

- Library and bookstore people, especially independent booksellers.

- Other published writers and would-be writers of your acquaintance.

- Town dignitaries and politicos of note.

- Business associates or others with whom you do business, particularly those for whom you are an important customer. The printer, typesetter, artists, etc., from whom you bought services in getting your book out are prime candidates.

- Always address your invitation to both husband and wife,

Notes

Any reading, program or other activity that you take part in is ammunition for your news release program. Do not hesitate to fire off a release whenever the occasion warrants. Even the briefest mention in your newspaper—whether in a business note section, a community calendar section, or even the social page—is important in building your image as a successful, published poet. Sample news releases for a variety of occasions are given in the text. Study these, then go and do likewise.

59

in the case of married couples.

Be sure to cross-reference these lists to eliminate duplicates. Also eliminate names of individuals who, for one reason or another, you just don't want to show up at the affair. The names you have left will constitute your basic invitation list.

The Invitations Themselves

The invitations will be typeset and printed in a standard formal invitation format. This can be done inexpensively at most quick-copy shops that also feature desktop publishing typesetting.

An invitation that I have used frequently and successfully reads as follows:

> *Venture Press, Publishers*
> *and*
> *(name of co-sponsor)*
> *request the pleasure of your company*
> *at a reception and autograph signing*
> *honoring*
> *(author's name)*
> *on the occasion of*
> *the publication of (his, her) book,*
> *(name of book).*
> *(Date, written out)*
> *from five until seven in the evening*
> *at (location of party).*
>
> *Regrets only.*

Invitations will be mailed out approximately two weeks in advance. This is not the kind of event anyone is likely to postpone a vacation trip for, so you want it to arrive close enough to the date of the event to be easily remembered.

Regrets only are solicited so that those who would otherwise have forgotten to respond to an RSVP will feel free to stop by for congratulations and a glass of wine or a cocktail.

The News Release

You will send a news release to the social editor and to the book editor (if any) of your local newspaper telling of the upcoming

Notes

event. Your goal is to get it reported as a social event of importance just a few days before the party itself— preferably on the preceding Sunday. This article will serve to remind those who received invitations of the time and place of the event, and it will serve to enhance the event and increase attendance at it.

The Best Time of Day

What is the best time for your autograph party? Well, you want both husband and wife to attend, if possible. You don't want to conflict with more (to the guest) important social commitments. You want to fit in easily with personal schedules.

I have found that an event scheduled from five until seven or seven-thirty, on a week-day night, works best. Of the available week-days experience shows that Tuesday and Thursday work best. The time slot is easily manageable. Business persons can stop by on the way home from work, dressed in their business clothes. Wives and husbands can easily meet at the party location. And the time commitment is limited enough to reassure anyone that the event, though pleasant enough, is not likely to monopolize their evening.

Correctly organized, however, and with a good mix of guests, autograph parties have a way of becoming more enjoyable than most imagined they would be, and guests linger longer (and buy more books) than they expected to.

The Best Location

While a friend who is sponsoring your party may be quite willing to have it in her home, this may not be the best choice. I have found that some public place, preferably arts-related, works better than a private residence.

I think this is true because individuals who simply want to drop in can do so more easily when the autograph party is taking place in a public place. They do not feel as obliged to go home from work, and shower and change as they would if attending a cocktail party in a large private home. Attendance will be greater. Such a location, too, helps focus attention on you as poet and allays any reservations an individual might have about the promotional aspects of the evening. In the absence of other available locations, however, a quite successful evening can be planned at a home.

What kind of public place? I recommend that arrangements be made to have the event in the reception area, say, of the local

Notes

museum of art or in the facilities of the local arts council. In your area other such locations may be possible. You may also consider renting space, if it is affordable, in a local hotel or motel, but I would do this only if nothing else was available and if the space itself was often used by the community for receptions and similar events.

Keep the area as small as you can relative to the number of people you expect to serve. (No more that 50% of those invited, in all likelihood, will attend.) It is far better to have more people in a smaller space than the same number of guests lost in the expanse of a ballroom.

The Physical Arrangements

Do not spread out over too large an area. Provide a table of attractive but affordable hors d'oeuvres somewhere near the center of the area where you wish the bulk of the guests to congregate. To one side you will position a table where someone will serve white wine or perhaps simple cocktails, depending on your personal tastes and budget. But it is important to have one or the other of these beverages. Punch will be available for the non-drinkers present.

Not too distant from the food and drink—but far enough away to be perceived as a separate center of attention—will be a table on which your books are stacked, along with a poster board and easel with an enlargement of the cover, quotes from reviewers and perhaps a "Congratulations" banner of some kind. This table will be the center of book sales as the reception progresses. Someone will be present at this table at all times to handle the money, make change, etc. You do not want to do this yourself. The sales table should be positioned so that guests leaving the party will be aware of its presence, since they will have to pass close by.

Another small table will be set up with a single chair. At this table you will sign books purchased by the guests and brought to you. Most writers sign on the title page, near the place where their name is printed. Always ask for whom the book is being bought, and be sure to check the spelling of unfamiliar names. You can sign simply, "Best wishes to _____", followed by your name and the date.

The Signing and the Selling

At about six or six fifteen (if you started up at five) the crowd

Notes

will peak before starting to thin out a little. At this moment the host will get the attention of the crowd, welcome the guests and thank them for coming, tell about you and your book (using information you have provided) and offer a toast. You will respond, briefly. Your host will then announce that you will be available to autograph this *first edition* (this phrase has strong sell-power) of your books as they are brought to you. Then she bids the guests to continue the celebration.

At this point you have to let the guests know what to do. For most if not all of them this will be the first autograph party they have been to. *They will not know what is expected of them. You will have to show them by example.* Arrange for several friends to purchase copies (real purchases or not) at this time. They need to pull out the bucks and get change so that others will know what is to be done. Then they will take their books to you for signing. After the signing they will proudly show their copy off to other guests at the party.

All this can be done quite naturally, and it is absolutely essential to initiate the process of getting book sales going.

Bookstore Parties

Occasionally you see an ad for a bookstore autograph signing. An author will be present to sign copies of books bought there by customers. These sometimes work, at the right place and time, and with a very well-known author. But they are a great gamble, and usually fail to attract the crowds that you need to be successful.

Nobody is free to go by the store during business hours, and in the late afternoon, when all the world is at home enjoying an end-of-the-day cocktail, who wants to go to a shopping mall to watch some poet sign a book?

And there's nothing lonelier than an autograph party to which no one comes.

My advice is to avoid bookstore autograph parties unless you are very well-known in the community and unless the community is a very unusual one it its support of literature and the arts. I might try it in a bookstore on Harvard Square or in downtown Chapel Hill, but unless I was supported by a folk singer, a band and a group of ethnic dancers I would not count on success even them.

Notes

On success in the business of literature.... We are social animals and we create ourselves in the eyes of others. The gaze of others defines us, socially and professionally speaking. We must take reasonable care that others see us and think about us as we would wish to be seen and thought about.

Pictured below are the front and back of a business reply card that I use to generate requests for review copies. I send the book itself and a media kit to the major review sources and a media kit and reply card to the many more or less marginal review sources.

_____

_____

Place
Stamp
Here

Marketing Manager
Venture Press
104 South Respess Street
Washington, NC 27889

YES, please send me a complimentary review copy of your book HOW TO PUBLISH YOUR POETRY: THE FIRST-EVER MARKETING MANUAL AND SUCCESS GUIDE FOR POETS.

Please mail to:

Name _____

Street_____

City _____Zip _____

For possible review in _____

Chapter 8

How to Give Great Poetry Readings

Make no mistake about it, a poetry reading is—or should be—a full-scale, carefully planned performance of which you are the star. The more you make it one the more successful you will be.

Unfortunately these powerful marketing tools for poetry are almost always misused or not really used at all, and that is a dreadful waste.

You have everything going for you. The audience is always friendly and well-disposed toward you. They have, after all, chosen to come to this place to meet you and listen to you read your own work. Some are poets themselves; some are lovers of poetry; some are friends who have come along to show their support for you.

They are here because they want to talk poetry, hear poetry, think poetry, meet at least one successful poet (you) and exchange ideas about their craft. They will gather any crumbs of gratification (usually all they will get at most readings) offered to them and leave very grateful for having gotten anything at all.

"He who has a thing to sell,
And goes and whispers in a well,
Is not so apt to get the dollars,
As he who climbs a tree and
hollers."

—Anonymous, quoted by
Barbara Brabec in her book,
Homemade Money

Why the Starvation Diet?

Why keep them on this starvation diet so lacking in all the good things they desire? Why not serve them up a rich, double helping of goodies instead?

Your audience deserves a good show and you, as author of the poems being read, certainly deserve a good show. More than that, you *need* it. *But unless you take charge and make it happen, neither you nor your audience is likely to enjoy the promised feast.* For the sad fact is that poetry readings are typically deadly dull. And this is quite a paradox. A poet uses language to achieve the most intense possible communication and yet the evening's readings are most often devoid of life, let alone passion.

Something Different

The challenge is to make your own readings something different, something above and beyond the ordinary. A reading is, after all, a performance and you are the chief performer. Think of a favorite play. When inexperienced people sit around in a circle and read the text in low-keyed voices, the sparks do not fly, the tinder does not catch and the fire does not begin to burn. But let fine actors utter those same words in the context of a production and the heart begins to race. Something important is happening, and the spectators are caught up in it.

An Art That Can Be Learned

You need to convert your readings, insofar as you can, into a performance that will catch your listeners up in the same way. Most of us are not natural performers. Fortunately, putting on a dramatic reading is an art that can be learned. As you work at developing your reading and as you do more and more of them you will become more and more adept at achieving the kind of powerful communication you want. Your poetry is art. But your reading of it is *showbiz*.

Molding Audience Expectations

The psychologists talk about "mind-set." They use these words to refer to the mental and emotional *expectation* in individuals and groups that predisposes them to react to what they see and hear in

Notes

66

a particular way. This is one of the great secrets of show business. Everything about a successful performance, all the peripherals and props, must predispose the audience to think "This is great!." And that is what they do think. They are predisposed to enjoy, to approve, to applaud.

A typical rock music concert provides a wonderful example. What is the reality of it? Rather unattractive young performers stalk about the stage with unpleasant expressions on their faces, shouting bad lyrics to worse music. The music itself is performed with mediocre skill by musicians of somewhat limited talent. Yet thousands of spectators stand, cheer and otherwise carry on as though in utter ecstasy of artistic enjoyment.

The Packaging Makes the Product

With rare exceptions it is the packaging rather than the product that provokes this frenzied response. The mind-set is carefully prepared to facilitate it.

There are only five or six musicians and singers performing on the stage. Yet the day before legions of lighting specialists, sound technicians, stage hands and others have arrived with truckloads of paraphernalia and props—enough to make the magic screen of the Wizard of Oz look like a child's sparkler by comparison. Smoke rises from the stage, electronic fireworks illuminate the vast auditoriums, sound systems capable of deafening a major modern city amplify beyond all imagining the lead singer's clumsiest stroking of his guitar. The excitement is palpable. It is not just a concert; it is an *experience*.

Well, of course, you may not be ble to match that act. But you can and must learn from it. Always keep in mind that the atmosphere of your reading is as important as the reading itself. If you want your audience to listen to you and to react enthusiastically to your verse (and buy your book) you've got to work to create an environment that encourages them to do so.

The fact is that most people don't know what to do at a poetry readings—including, in most cases, the poet. At a basketball game, when a player makes an unbelievably deft move and scores a key basket, you stand up and cheer. But when a poet turns out a near perfect line or passes through one of those "sudden rightnesses" that great poetry is made of, what's to do? Shout "Yeah!" as they do at jazz concerts?

Exactly. That is precisely the kind of reaction one should encourage. Yet the atmosphere of most readings is more like that of

> Notes

> *"A poet who doesn't have a book of his own along to take orders on when he's giving a reading isn't a serious poet, because he really doesn't want to share his work with the people who come in contact with it. Every poet should therefore always have a book which...he can take orders for, either by himself or via a friend by the entrance table ....Remember, the old meaning of publish is proclaim. Well, proclaim then. If you have something to say or to show, say it or show it to all who will listen. That, not false modesty, is real professionalism."*
>
> —Dick Higgins
> Something Else Press

afternoon tea at the Ladies' Missionary Society. Any show of real emotion is out of place. The atmosphere is not one of freedom but of inhibition.

You Can Change All That

You've got to work to change that. It may be a tall order, but you can do it. As you do more and more readings—of your own poetry and perhaps even the poetry of others—you will get better and better at it and have more and more fun. Those who come will truly enjoy themselves, and create a reputation and positive public visibility for you that will be an asset for years to come.

How are you going to accomplish all this? Here are some steps that will get you started along the way.

Be Aggressive in Lining Up Readings

Line up as many readings as you can. In the beginning explore every possibility, no matter how modest the opportunity. The first few readings are like a shakedown cruise. You get everything running right and coordinated. You learn your performer's craft.

In order to accomplish this you will want to do the following things:

- Utilize the same media kit that you used for your newspaper and TV publicity in building a schedule of readings. Send it to program chairpersons, then follow up with a telephone call.

- In each news article about your activities and in each TV appearance get the word out that you do readings.

- Approach writer's clubs, arts councils, public schools, community colleges, junior colleges, four-year colleges and universities and other special organizations whose interests may coincide with the themes in your poetry.

- If your poetry is religious in nature, for instance, church groups may be interested in having you.

- Let those responsible for program planning know that you are ready, willing and able to put on a superior performance at a moment's notice.

Notes

- Stress the fact that your readings go beyond the ordinary and create enthusiastic audience response and active audience participation. *Let them know that, more than a simple reading, your appearance will be an educational experience, a performance.*

- Treat each of these readings with all the care and professionalism that you can muster.

Take Charge

There are sayings that have been around for years. They have been around and are still around because they are very, very true. One is that "if you want something done right you have to do it yourself." Another comes from management seminars on small business. "Nobody", this saying goes, "cares about your business the way you do."

You will do well to take both these pieces of advice to heart. As soon as you have a reading lined up get in touch with the program chairperson. Find out who is responsible for getting the space ready for your appearance. Write up a paragraph or two outlining your needs, props, etc. for the chairperson's use. Offer your help in arranging things the way you want them.

Create Powerful Publicity

One of the most important parts of taking charges is to make sure that publicity plans are well-made, well-scheduled and as effective as possible.

- Remember that your program chairperson is no PR person and probably knows very little about publicizing an event beyond, maybe, putting a little note in an organization newsletter.

- If there is to be such a note, *you* write it for your program chairperson. Fill it with the kind of information that will attract more attendees. Build excitement and anticipation. Let people know that your reading will be something out of the ordinary and not to be missed.

- Send news releases announcing your appearance (and afterward, telling about it) to the local newspaper and to local radio and television stations.

Notes

- Offer to appear on their shows with some teasers from your performance.

- If possible organize a telephone campaign to contact persons who might be interested in coming.

- Contact English teachers and ask that your program be announced in class. Perhaps it could be made the subject of a theme or paper.

- If the organization's budget—or your own budget—can stand it send out invitations to a selected guest list.

I have said this before and I will say it again: nothing happens by itself. You have to make it happen. Remember that no one is as interested in your success as you are. What is your program chairperson's chief concern? That the program not bomb. Convince the chairperson that you simply will not stand for anything less that a smashing success and that the glory will be his as well as yours.

Create a Usable Space

Visit the premises several days before your performance. Allow yourself plenty of time to set things up (arrange the stage!) to suit you. Make certain that the room itself is warm and conducive to direct communication as possible. Often you may scout around the building and suggest that another location might be much more effective for your presentation. Decide where you want the lectern located, where the easels and other props go, where the refreshment table is to be located and where your table of books for autographing will be.

You do not want too few people to rattle around in a large space. You don't want to be cramped, but it is better to come close to filling up your space than have yawning gaps of emptiness to fill up with your energy. Water boils fastest in a small container; the steam whistles quickest from a small teapot. The same dynamic relationship between space and energy holds true between performancers and the space they work in.

Remember That You Are Planning a Performance

Plan your evening as though you were planning a perfor-

Notes

mance—which, whether you admit it or not, is just what you *are* doing. Good performances are well-organized performances. Don't wing it. Don't trust to luck and improvise as you go. Have the presentation well-planned. Develop specific answers to question such as these:

• When do I arrive?

• What am I going to say as I mingle with the audience during the social hour that will set the stage for my reading?

• Who will introduce me?

• What should they say as a good lead in?

• Which pieces will I read, and in what order so that I build to a climax?

• How do I get the audience involved?

• What do I say in closing?

• How do I let the audience know in the most effective way that I am available to autograph my books?

Every good dramatic performance, as Aristotle taught two thousand and more years ago, has a beginning, a middle and an end. It builds slowly, reaches a climax and then comes to a strong and satisfactory conclusion. Your reading must do the same thing.

Call On Friendly (and Free) Consultants in Staging and Drama

The one-man show has had a strong run of success on the stage in recent years: Hal Holbrook as Mark Twain and James Whitmore as Harry Truman are two examples from a few years back that come to mind.

What makes such shows successful? Find out and utilize these techniques yourself. If you have a friend in a community theater or an acquaintance who has experience in stage direction, consult them. If you don't know such people perhaps you can find them. Go to the local arts council, community college or even the high school English department. Odds are you can find people who are

---

Notes

Writer's block got you down? I suffered an acute case for many years. As a writer I was my own worst enemy. Then I read Dorothea Brande, where I found this simple bit of advice. "Act as though it were impossible to fail," Dorothea advised. For years, like some malevolently negative parrot perched on my own shoulder, I constantly fed messages into my ear. "You call that writing?", I would say to myself. Or, "That's the sorriest stuff I ever saw." Or, "Nobody in his right mind would call that poetry." Naturally, this didn't help at all. Then I began to play Dorothea Brande's game. I didn't have to believe it, I simply had to act as though I believed it. I began to write as though it were impossible not to write good, strong lines. And you know what?

I began to write more of them than I had ever been able to do before.

ready and willing to help with suggestions and ideas. It is a challenge, and it can be fun to bring it off. The question you put to your informal consultants is straightforward: "How can I make a poetry reading a dramatic success?" Gather as many ideas as you can, collate and sort them and use the ones that work best for you.

Every Detail is Important

Everything is important: what you wear, how you look, your tone of voice and the way you project it, the clarity of your diction and the expressiveness with which you read. Some rehearsal is definitely called for. Your expert-friend-consultant can furnish important feedback here.

Before the Reading

You will have taken care that the room is completely set up according to your instructions before the audience arrives. If necessary you will do this yourself.

- The refreshment table will be in place. Refreshments will be served both before and after the reading.

- Your autograph table is nearby, with stacks of books and display boards as we described above for autograph parties.

- As people begin to come in mingle with them and introduce yourself. Ask what *they* are doing and listen attentively. Have someone nearby who can spot key attendees and introduce you whenever possible.

- Do not socialize too long at this time. Allow the crowd to assemble, have a glass of wine and shake your hand.

- Then you wind your way to the front of the room where you are to do your reading. No later than five minutes after the announced time for the beginning, you begin.

As the Evening Begins

There are some important preliminaries to attend to before the reading itself begins.

Notes

- An introduction must be carefully done—so carefully, in fact, that you can't just leave it up to the program chairperson, who probably has no idea how to go about it. You will write and give to the chairperson an introductory script. It can then be read or, if the chairperson is at ease in front of an audience, paraphrased.

- You must let the audience know what the overall organization of the evening will be—that you will give your reading and that afterwards refreshments will be served. During that time you will hope to meet with everyone present and answer all questions and "just have fun talking about writing and publishing poetry."

- The introducer will also announce that you will be available to autograph your books.

- The introducer (or you) will let the audience know who you are and what you have written. If you have published widely, mention some of the more impressive publications. If there are reviews, the introducer can quote these so long as it is done in good spirits and in a low key. Many of those present will be poets (in fact or in their dreams) and will enjoy hearing about your professional trials, tribulations and triumphs so long as this is done in the right spirit of fun.

Down with Victorian Restraint!

Let the audience know that this is going to be a reading unlike others that they may have attended. Let them know that you welcome interaction, questions—even interruptions. Let them know that it is OK to make noise, to clap, whistle, shout encouragement, boo and hiss—that it is OK to have fun with poetry.

I have often been struck by the fact that at poetry readings there seems to be no socially acceptable audience reaction other than polite, Victorian restraint. The poet finishes reading a piece and is met by dead silence. He has no idea where he stands with the audience. If they like it, silence. If they don't like it, silence. If they don't understand it, silence. And on to the next page. It is only their love of poetry that keeps them (mostly) awake.

This just won't do. I have often—and very seriously—thought of giving out Halloween noisemakers at the door. As stirring passages are read appropriate sounds of approval can be made by

Another bit of advice that has been immensely helpful to me: You can't create and criticize simultaneously. When you're constantly criticizing every word you put down on the page you simply stifle the free flow of words, images and rhythms. To act otherwise is like trying to water the daisies when there's a kink in the hose. There's plenty of water in the underground reservoir but only a dribble comes out the nozzle. Now shake the kink out and water flows freely. That's what happens when you give up your habit of constant self criticism. Time enough to exercise your critical faculties after you get the first draft down on paper.

shaking, swinging, whirling or blowing into the devices furnished to the audience. Certainly it would impress on those attending that I was serious in inviting their reaction. It could work very nicely.

Warm Them Up

When you watch a live show on television—a comedy show like *Tonight* or even a quiz show, the host always walks out to thunderous applause as the show begins. How, you may ask, could a cold audience reach such a pitch of enthusiasm in so short a time. The answer is that the audience is not cold at all. For an hour or more it has been warmed up, carefully primed for the moment you have just witnessed.

How can you warm your audience up? Here are some random ideas that will illustrate the kind of thing that I am talking about and that is needed. These fit my personality. Others will occur to you that fit yours.

- Kick things off on a light vein, establishing a tone of fun and relaxed interplay for the evening. You might try something like a humorous introduction to the kinds of silence that universally befall poets at their readings. Then you may suggest what you think can be done about it and lead the audience in practicing boos and cheers and in using their noisemakers.

- Read sure-fire zingers from other poets—parts of Whitman's *Song of Myself,* for instance. Such poetry can be fairly shouted out at an audience and ought to be greeted with shouts of approval and choruses of "Right-on's." Lead the cheers yourself. Also include some dismal stuff that you can all hiss and boo.

- Then read other well-known poems to indicate the range of reaction possible. Read difficult poems. Read them first as though you assume everyone understands. Then hand out a sheet with the poem printed on it and read again. Stress that poems are made with words, rhythms and sounds but also with the semantic properties of those sounds. So we may get more from it when we follow the text, at least the first time, with our eyes, especially when the poem is dense or difficult.

Notes

- Ask questions of your audience. Point at them. Jump up and down and yell at them if necessary, but get them involved.

Develop Your Own Patter

A stand-up performer continually talks to the audience, whetting its appetite, building its interest, heightening its reaction to the next part of the act.

I loved to go down to the stage shows that they used to put on at the old Bijou theatre in downtown Savannah when I was a boy. My favorites were the performances of the sleight-of-hand magicians. These old-time troupers would stand alone on the stage, perhaps with the help of a single assistant, sometimes with no help at all. They would surround the act of magic with constant talk. They would tell about first discovering the next marvel in the mysterious east. They would make us keenly aware of the difficulties of accomplishing a particularly complicated feat, such that we appreciated it all the more when it actually happened. They would entertain and amuse us with anecdotes and stories as the evening wore on.

A poet is a magician, too—a magician of words—and effective patter is just as necessary to his own act as any other.

What kind of patter? You will discover bits and pieces of it as you gain experience. For instance:

- Introduce each poem fully.

- Tell stories that let the audience see you as a human being struggling to find expression for a feeling, emotion or experience that is particularly important to you.

- Tell them about the technical problems you encountered and how you solved them.

- You may find it useful to provide copies of any difficult pieces you are going to read or of any that you are going to use as examples in your talk.

- Understand that when you skip this patter and proceed to read your poems without the necessary introduction they are over before the audience has begun even to focus its attention on the piece you are reading. You lose the audience before you begin. The reading of a lyric poem is a little like

Notes

"Doing business without advertising is like winking at a girl in the dark. You know what you are doing but nobody else does."

—*S.H. Britt*

the Kentucky Derby. The race itself is over in a matter of minutes. It's the preliminaries that make the Derby the event that it is.

- Sprinkle your presentation with talk of other poets that you know and their own challenges and triumphs.

- Tell humorous—or otherwise—stories of how you got started and how you published your first bit of verse in that grade school newspaper.

- The more personal and direct your patter, the more warmly involved your listeners become and the more effective your reading will be.

As you do more and more readings, your patter will become more and more effective. You try new things, keep the ones that work best and discard the others.

Develop Your Own "Stump Speech"

Politicians who tour the country during electoral campaigns develop what they call a stump speech. Since they obviously cannot prepare a new talk for each of the scores of stops along their way, they develop one presentation that is slightly altered to suit individual groups and circumstances.

The presentation you develop is your poetical stump speech. You do not have to create a new presentation each time you go out. Instead you keep refining the materials you have developed. Stick with what works best. You might use different anecdotes for grade school, high school and university audiences, but the overall performance will be the same.

There will come a time when a dangerous illusion sets in. You have done your routine so often that you will feel that others must have heard it as many times as you have and become bored with it. If this were true every broadway play, even the best, would close after the first month. This is a common but mistaken feeling among those who appear frequently in public. Remember that for your audience your presentation is as fresh as the dew and that your only challenge is to remain as enthusiastic and involved as they are.

Notes

These Techniques Will Work for You

Everything I say in this chapter, all the techniques I recommend, will work. I know this because I have used them all. Most important, however, is the principal of the thing: *a poetry reading must be treated as a performance.*

There are certainly different approaches that will work, and many that may work very well for you when they would not for me or anyone else. These grow out of your special talents and interests. Maybe you will strum on a guitar while you read your verse. Maybe you will appear in costume. Maybe you will get the audience involved in creating an instant poem through games like the surrealists' "Exquisite Corpse" (Cadavre exquis), where nouns, verbs, exclamations, etc., are written down by the assembled group on separate scraps of paper and a poem is made by drawing them out of hats as needed. The results can often be extraordinary in their creation of powerful and astonishing imagery.

But whatever you do, your fame and name will spread, and, if you work persistently to schedule readings and then to do them with drama and flair, you will begin a gratifying career of writing, publishing and selling your poems. And, wonder of wonders, you may even begin to make money. The fact that you treat your readings as performances will have put you in a class apart.

Sell Your Poems

After the reading you will have created a spirited and pleased group of new friends. When the performance is over many of them will gather around the "back of the room" table where you have spread out your books to continue the fun, to discuss poetry and to stretch the evening as much as possible.

You will, of course, want to sell some books. Again the path of wisdom is to have a friend make the first purchase to let the others know just how to go about it. The sponsors of the reading can be recruited to make change. You can also do this yourself, but it is difficult to carry on conversations, autograph books and make change at the same time.

You should take steps to optimize your sales and your profits. The attitude that poetry is a genteel activity not to be sullied by mere money is widespread—and it is as strange as it is wrong. Do you not like to eat? Do you not travel, buy books, give Santa to the kids at Christmas?

You can offer other books for sale as well as your own. "How to" titles (like this one, for instance) can be bought from their publishers at discounts ranging from 40 to 50 percent, usually depending on the quantities purchased.

This book, *How to Publish Your Poetry,* sells for $24.95 in its ring-binder edition. You can buy copies from the publisher at wholesale for $14.95 in quantities of ten or more. The books of all other major publishers can be bought on roughly the same terms. Local, independent publishers may let you have books on consignment without your having to buy them. The discount, however, is likely to be less.

The difference between your purchase price and the retail price that you sell them for is your profit.

Talk to your audience about these books. Work some mention of them naturally into your presentation. Describe how and in what ways they have been valuable to you. You cannot help but sell some of them at each reading. When you are firmly established you might arrange with your bank to offer charge card service.

You might also offer audio cassettes of your own presentations and the presentations of others, which you will purchase and sell on the same discount terms.

Notes

Chapter 9

How To Publish It Yourself

There are far more deserving poets than there are presses to publish them. The number of small and independent publishers—though greater than you ever imagined—is still very small when compared to the number of good books submitted to them. I can imagine poems of true excellence tucked away in attics all over America because their authors failed, not as poets but as marketers of poems.

Mark Twain tells the story of an individual who, having gone to heaven, witnessed a celestial parade of the greatest poets in history. At the head of the file, just in front of Homer and Dante, marched a little shoemaker from the backwoods of Tennessee. He was the greatest of them all. He just never managed to get published.

So Do It Yourself

Today there is a sure way, once and for all, to end your own frustration at writing good poems that you can't get into print. You can publish and sell them yourself. Bear in mind the fact that the only books of verse that are likely to be sold are those the poet himself sells to relatives and friends, to local libraries and to the general public at personal appearances and readings.

"Always keep your design simple. Readability is the primary consideration. And never forget that the poem itself is the star of the show. Fancy layouts often just confuse the reader and cost the publisher a ton of money that he would be better off spending on something else."

—*Thomas A. Williams,*
in How to Make
$100,000 a Year in
Desktop Publishing.

79

Such things are as easy to arrange when you publish your book yourself as when someone else does it for you. Plus you have total control over the design of your book and you get to keep *all* the money you make when you sell a copy.

Though no one is likely to get rich writing poetry, self-published authors of verse often recoup all their expenses and make a modest profit if they are willing to do the necessary marketing.

There Are Many Ways to Profit

When you publish, after all, you do not measure profit solely in terms of the money you make from direct book sales. There are other very real sources of benefit. While it is true that a book of poetry, with the help of the poet in promotion, can sell well enough to pay expenses, it certainly will not do much too more than that. Still, to get those poems out of your desk drawer and into the world of published literature can be of immense value by projecting the author onto an entirely new level of professional achievement and literary visibility.

Beyond the immense personal satisfaction that publication will bring, the greater visibility often translates itself into invitations to give lectures and talks, participate in arts council planning and decisions, work in the schools, and more. Such assignments often bring welcome stipends and honoraria along with them.

If you are a teacher, publication can bring a merit raise in salary which will multiply itself month after month and year after year, earning you more money than royalties on book sales could ever do. It will also bring all the benefits of professional recognition, facilitate promotion and otherwise enhance your career.

Some years ago my book on the French poet Stephane Mallarme was published by the University of Georgia Press. This book had a total market of about 600 university libraries in this country and in Europe, and that is just about the number of copies my book sold.

There was no way that the University of Georgia Press could make a cent on the project, and my own royalties amounted to less that $200. Nevertheless, I profited handsomely. Overnight I was transformed from an unknown assistant professor into an established scholar. I got a promotion to the rank of associate professor. I got better classes to teach. My salary was raised substantially, and over a twenty year period I can trace more than $100,000 of increased earnings (via higher salaries) to the publication of that one

Notes

book.

It's OK to Self-Publish

In case there's any lingering doubt in your mind concerning the legitimacy of self-publication, let me take a moment here to set the record straight. Writers and others who have not been following the truly revolutionary changes in the publishing industry in the last few years may not be aware of the way in which the landscape has changed.

Almost twenty years ago now, Bill Henderson, founder of Pushcart Press, self-published his *The Publish-It-Yourself Handbook: Literary Tradition and How-to*. This book was a rousing success and sold edition after edition nationwide. It is still on bookstore shelves and going strong—so strong, in fact that the sales of this one title were adequate to build Henderson's one- man enterprise into one of the great success stories in the independent publishing movement of recent years.

Henderson was a man before his time. When he wrote his *Handbook*, the technology that has made publishing absurdly easy for anyone who truly wishes to get into print had not even been invented. So the how-to part of his book is somewhat dated.

The literary tradition section, however, did a very great service for the whole independent publishing movement. Henderson pointed out that self-publication had a long and noble history. Walt Whitman, Carl Sandburg, Stephen Crane, Edgar Allen Poe, and dozens of the greatest names in our literature all self-published at one time or another.

Far from being a back-door entry into the world of published poets, self-publication today is booming and is *very* respectable. As money becomes tighter and as the big publishers focus more and more exclusively on the quest for the million dollar best seller, it has become inescapably clear that for books with limited sales potential—as all books of verse clearly are—self-publication is not only an acceptable alternative but often the *only* alternative.

The writing of books, manuals and guides for self-publishing writers has itself become a mini-industry within the the publishing field. Judith Applebaum, a long-time pro in the New York publishing field, has a book on the market called *How to Get Happily Published*. Applebaum's book is one of the best on the subject that I have ever read. It tells the fiction and non-fiction writer how to approach the big commercial houses, outlines strategies for getting careful readings from thoughtful editors, and much more. The

Occasionally you will be asked for permission to reprint one or more of your poems. My advice is that the name recognition will be useful to you and that you should willingly accede to the request. However, always specify the precise wording of the credit line you require. Don't forget to let the reader know where your book can be ordered and how to reach you. For example: "That Certain Summer", copyright 1991 by Jane Doe. Reprinted by permission of Jane Doe from Collected Poems of Jane Doe, Orpheus Press, 200 W. Second Street, Anytown, USA,

significant thing is that the last section of the book is devoted to the how-to of self-publication. This New York pro has no hesitation in treating self-publication as a perfectly feasible and totally acceptable alternative for many writers.

Dan Poynter, founder of Para Books, has written *The Self-Publishing Manual* , the most complete—and virtually indispensable—step-by-step instruction manual on self-publishing available today. Another of his titles, *Publishing Short-Run Books* takes you through the actual hands-on process of putting your book together and getting it ready for the printer.

Where most such books fall short, however, is that they deal primarily with non-fiction titles. Still, the basic information they contain is solid and valid, and they are indispensable reading for anyone considering self-publication.

If you believe in your book and want to see it in print, bring it out yourself, utilizing the methods and strategies that I will outline in the following sections. Take this route and your book will be published. It will no longer languish, unread, in your desk drawer. It will be out in the world, on its own, where it will stand alongside other books of its kind on its own merits.

Self-Publisher's Checklist

Is your book of poetry a good candidate for self-publication? To find out, study the following checklist. You should be able to answer "yes" (even a qualified yes will do) to most of these questions:

- Does your poetry meet at least one or two of the criteria for publishable poetry outlined in Chapter 2?

- Are you willing to make the necessary effort to follow the production and design guidelines specified in Chapter 10?

- Are you willing to study and implement the marketing techniques specified in Chapter 6?

- Are you willing to schedule and give readings of your verse?

- Are you willing to accept the fact that the very best you can do financially is make a modest profit on direct sales of your book?

Notes

Ok, did you pass the test? If so, let's go on and see just how it is done.

Name your publishing company.

You may be a self-publisher, but the operative word is still publisher. Open any book on your shelf and look at the title page. You will see the title, the author's name and the name of the publishing company (the "imprint", as it is called).

Harper & Row, Simon & Schuster, Alfred A. Knopf....all these are imprints, as are hundreds of other publisher's names.

When your book comes out you will want it to look, feel and *be* just like the products of any other publishing company. You will have to choose a name for your own imprint. You can be whimsical, poetical or whatever you like, but keep the following points in mind.

- Do not name your company after yourself. Your name will already be on the title page as author. Don't double up as publishing company name too. "My Book of Poems" by Sue Smith, Sue Smith Press is just too much of a good thing. Choose something else. There are several good reasons for this. When you see how well your own book goes you may want to branch out and publish the work of other poets. They would probably prefer to have the work appear over a neutral imprint rather than one promoting your own name. They will want, and probably deserve, to be the only poet listed on the title page.

- If your work is regional in tone, you may want to choose a regional-sounding name: Copper Canyon, North Point, Tar River Press are some successful ones that come to mind. Such regional imprints will attract the attention of reviewers for regional newspapers and magazines. The regional name gives them an immediate reason to pick up and browse through your book. If they like it, perhaps they will write about it. After all, being up on literary activity in their geographical area is part of their job.

- Whatever you do, don't choose a name that belittles your newborn publishing company. I don't think I would go for "Last Chance Press" or "Better Than Nothing Books", for instance. Yet you would be surprised just how many people

Notes

"Be willing to do interviews with newspaper reporters from smaller newspapers. Very often, as a matter of fact, a well-written press release will be printed verbatim by a smaller newspaper....They must fill each issue of their newspaper. If your material is good and does not require a lot of editing...you stand a good chance of them running your material, especially if you've sent along a lively photograph."

—*Peggy Glenn, in* Publicity for Books and Authors

do precisely that.

Eschew Self-Deprecation—Now and Evermore

Many writers—modest souls that they are—play the game of self-deprecation for all that it is worth. They play it to the point of doing themselves and their reputations real damage. Or, if not damage, then very little good. I know, because I used to suffer from this affliction myself—and still do, to some extent, when I am not careful.

When your book comes out, you immediately become that *avis rara* the published poet. Smile. Beam. Give interviews. Take yourself seriously. Remember that it is a given of human nature: people, in forming opinions about us, take their cues from us. If we take ourselves seriously, so will they. If we don't do so, then there's little chance that anyone else will, either.

You have put all of your talent, your heart and your soul into writing the poems that you have published. Why then, would you be tempted, when asked to sign a book, "Well, if you really want me to." Or why, when handing someone your book to look at, would you be tempted to say, "This is just a little book of my poems", hang your head to the side and smile uncertainly.

I don't know why, but I do know that many writers suffer from a self-effacement syndrome so serious as to rob themselves of all believability. Remember than for others, particularly for non-writers, you, as a published author, are almost a mythic figure. Play the part. Be what you are—a writer and a darn good one. Such a demeanor sells books and, besides, it is a lot of fun. The old ego can use a little admiration from time to time.

Take Pains With Book Design

Take great pains to design a book that does justice to your work. Appearances are important. Happily, your book can be both handsome and affordable. Details on how to accomplish this are given later. More about this in the next chapter.

Set Up As A Business

Get all the normal accouterments of business: business cards, letterhead, invoices, statements, etc. If you want people to do business with you you will have to be businesslike about it. And don't forget that as self-publisher, you are a businessperson. There will

Notes

be financial benefits to you, if only through tax savings, that are substantial. Your printing expenses, marketing expenses, travel on behalf of your book or in search of ideas, telephone, word-processor or computer, dues and subscriptions, travel to writer's and publisher's meetings and conventions and home office expense are tax deductible. If you are incorporated you, as president of your corporation, are eligible for goodies like before-tax medical and life insurance. Check with your accountant.

Establish A Marketing Program

Set up a formal marketing program to bring your book to the attention of the public. Study carefully the chapters "The Unabashed Poet's Guide to Self-Marketing", "How to Give an Autograph Party", and "How to Give the World's Best Poetry Readings." Make a one-two-three list of how you are going to accomplish all the things discussed in them. Schedule the implementation of this program in great detail. Make check lists to prod your memory. Do *what* you schedule yourself to do *when* you schedule yourself to do it. There will be a lot to do and without considerable self-organization you won't get it all done.

Is it important that you do so? Decidedly so, since *in the business of selling books nothing happens without marketing.* All this holds true whether you self-publish your book or whether someone else publishes for you. As a published poet who wants to sell his books you have no choice: you are your own marketing department.

If all of this marketing and business talk seems crassly commercial to you or beneath your dignity as a poet, you are wrong. Your judgment springs from a terrific naiveté. Even the finest writers actively market their books and blow their own horns. Do you think that Dylan Thomas really enjoyed traveling around from campus to campus reading his poems night after night. Do you think that writers actually take great pleasure in small town TV interviews and bad hotels on coast to coast tours. Not really. There is, of course, a flush of pleasure during the first heady days and weeks. After that, public appearances—with notable exceptions—become a job to be done. Writers do these things because they know that they must do them to make their books sell.

Notes

"A casebound book may cost anywhere from $2 to $3 more to produce than a paperback book. However, you can sell it for more than double the price of the paperback version."

—*Thomas A. Williams,* in How to Make $100,000 a Year in Desktop Publishing.

A printer's quote to Venture Press for the printing and binding of a 48 page book of poetry, perfect bound with a laminated 10 pt. cover.

Tom Williams
Venture Press
106 S. Respass Street
Washington, NC 27889

Re: ANSON COUNTY

We are pleased to submit our specifications and prices:

```
        QUANTITIES:  500; Add'l 100's
        TRIM SIZE:   6 x 9
        PAGES:       48
        COPY:        Text - camera ready repro's with 1 halftone without bleeds
                     Cover - camera ready mechanical
        PRESS:       Text - via offset lithography; black ink throughout
                     Cover - via offset lithography; covers 1, 4 & spine print black with
                     Duro Sheen
        STOCK:       Text - 60# Booktext Natural, 408 PPI
                     Cover - 10 pt. C1S
        PROOFS:      Text - complete bluelines
                     Cover - complete bluelines
        BINDING:     Saddle stitch on the 9" side
        PACKING:     Bulk pack in single wall RSC cartons on pallets
        SHIPPING:    FOB B/C dock, point of manufacturing
        TERMS:       Credit to be arranged
```

PRICES:	500	Add'l 100's
TOTAL:	$934	$33

Approximate freight from Chelsea, MI to Greenville, NC (27858): $65 Minimum charge

Thank you for the opportunity to submit our estimate. For your order, please call me at (313) 475-9145, extension 280.

Ed Blissick
Account Executive

EB/lh
cc: S. Ringler (BookMasters 1 800/537-6727)

Chapter 10

How to Design and Print a Book

Many poets may shy away from the publication of their own work not because they have any philosophical or financial reservations about the project but because they simply don't know how to go about it.

Their reluctance to take on the project is understandable. The whole process of book production is new to them. How much will it cost? What will the book look like? Who will print it? All of these basic questions rattle around in their heads and create great uncertainty.

Easier Than It Seems

Fortunately getting a book into print is much easier than it seems to those unfamiliar with the process. And while the first book you self-publish may require a bit of thought, preparation and even nervous sweat about the brow, those that follow will be a snap.

Your goal is to make a book that is both attractive and inexpensive to produce. You want it to look as good as or better than other

A very valuable reference for understanding the specialized vocabulary you will need in your dealings with printers and designers is the Pocket Pal: A Graphic Arts Production Handbook. This little book is copiously illustrated and very helpful. To obtain a personal copy write directly to the publisher: International Paper Co., International Paper Plaza, 77 W. 45th. Street, New York, NY, 10036. I highly recommend it to you.

Notes

books, but you don't want to mortgage the farm to get it done.

In the discussion that follows I will refer you to some other books that focus exclusively on the production process, so that if you feel that you require additional information you will know where to find it. I find these books fun to read, and often mine from them valuable nuggets of information. Those that I recommend are, in my opinion, the cream of the crop.

You can get started well enough with the basic information given in this chapter.

How to Design Your Book

A tried and true technique for the person with no experience in book layout and design is simply this: go to bookstores and libraries. Find a book whose appearance pleases you. Then make your own book look like the one you have chosen as a model.

I used this method quite successfully when I was a beginner in the publishing field. It's a little like learning to cook. As an amateur chef, I looked up recipes for the dishes I wanted to prepare and followed each step assiduously. As time went on I began to play around with the recipes. Today, I almost never consult them. I have learned the powers and potencies of the various spices and culinary techniques and I combine them at will. I do the same thing now with book design, except that the possible variations are far more limited in publishing than they are in the kitchen.

One of the easier, but more costly, ways to bring your book out is simply to take your sample book, along with your poems, to a local print shop. Once there you tell the printer, "Make my book look like this one." But, of course, this is a little like asking a contractor to build a house for you "like that one on the corner" without first exploring and nailing down costs. One of the most important things you will learn in this chapter is the necessity for shopping for price among printers.

When you design your book you will be making decisions on the following items, among others:

- **Page size.** Five and a half by eight and a half is the most flexible and generally affordable page size, although six by nine runs a close second. The smaller of these is the size of a normal piece of cut paper, the kind that you buy in reams for copy machines and for typing. That page size enables you to fold up and stitch (staple) together your book yourself. *Do not choose any non-standard page size.* Such a choice may present production difficulties and will surely cost you money.

- **Stock.** The work "stock" is used by printers to refer to the paper your book is printed on. Normally printers can match any stock samples you show them. They will have available booklets of various stocks that you can look through and choose among. If you are dealing with an out-of-town printer, which may very well be the case, ask them to send you samples of the papers that they use most frequently. Avoid fancy or unusual papers.

- **Type styles.** There are a great many styles of type available. You will want to choose a very straight-forward one that is easy to read. Avoid like the plague any fancy, script, "old-English" or other specialty types. The use of these type styles in a book is the sign of the amateur. The main thing wrong with them is that they are hard to read. Remember, at every stage of developing your book, that your poems themselves are the stars of the show. Do nothing to hinder access to them.

Ask the individual or company that is going to do your typesetting to give you a style sheet with the available type styles (called "fonts") shown on it. Choose the one that you find most readable. Some of the most desirable typestyles for use in books are:

- Times Roman

- Garamond

- Goudy Oldstyle

- Palatino

- Bookman

You will also be choosing some other aspects of type style. For instance, how big is the type? Type is measured in "points". For a book of verse I would recommend type no smaller than 10 points and no larger than 12. Ask to see samples. The space between the lines is called "leading" (rhymes with "bedding") and is usually specified 2 points greater than the size of the type style. Thus you might specify 10 point Garamond, with 12 point leading.

Notes

"...Be sure to keep the audience in mind and don't let your interviewer's questions or personality lead you away from the message you intend to deliver. Talk with or to the interviewer, but remember that your information is for all the listeners and viewers."

—*Peggy Glenn, in*
Publicity for Books and
Authors

If you simply show the person who is going to set your type a sample of the size you desire, he will be able to match it for you. Ask to have a single poem set in two or three sizes, then choose the one that you like best.

Other Design Elements

Studying the book you have chosen as a model, you will want to decide how you want the titles of each poem to appear. When you have more experience you can experiment. In the beginning you are far safer to follow someone else's successful example. A safe format, and one that I recommend, is to set the title set in italic type to contrast with the text of the poem, which is in roman (or "regular") type. Both the text and the title are flush left, that is, they are aligned on the left-hand margin.

Simple Is Better

In matters of design remember this basic rule: *simple and symmetrical is always better.*

- The page numbers have to go somewhere. Decide whether you want them in the outside corner of the page or at the center of the page.

- You will have to decide how you want the title page to appear. Again, when in doubt go with the symmetrical. There will be three items on the title page: the title itself, the author's name, and the name of the publishing company. (see samples)

- Other elements that you will have to decide on include the notice of copyright (in your own name, naturally), which is usually on the back of the title page, at the bottom.

- You will have a page of acknowledgments, including the names of the poems and publications in which any of the work in your book has previously appeared.

- You will have a dedication page. I usually do these flush right and ragged left, in italic.

- You will have a table of contents, alphabetically arranged.

Notes

• You may have a half title. Such pages include only the title of the book. They are the first printed page the reader comes to. When you turn past the half title you find the full title page before you. The half title is merely a device for utilizing an extra page which may be there because of the way your paper is folded.

How Many Pages?

Most books of poetry do not run too long. Forty-eight or 64 pages is a common length, with shorter chapbooks of 32 pages or even fewer not uncommon either. Your book will simply be long enough to contain the best poems that you have and that you want to publish.

Bear in mind, though, that because of the way paper is folded you will have to decide on a length that is a multiple of four, eight or sixteen. Books that are going to be produced by quick printers are done in multiples of four as are pages that you yourself will produce on a copy machine or run out on a laser printer.

A good question to ask your printer is this one: "What is the most cost effective length for this book?". You may find that because of the way the paper folds it is just as cheap to print a 64 page book as a 56 pager. Indeed I have seen cases where the 56 page book, cost *more* than one of 64 pages.

What Kind of Binding

There are two basic choices when it comes to deciding what kind of binding you want to give your book: paperbound and hardcover (casebound). Under paperbound there will be some sub-categories.

You will want to study additional, specialized reference books that go into great detail on matters of production. These books can be ordered through your bookstore or directly from the publisher. Some larger libraries will have copies on hand, or you can always obtain them through an inter-library loan request.

Your first project is a learning experience. After that you will discover that the book making and selling process is very straightforward and very simple, and you will seldom need any further advice. But you surely can, by following these instructions, do it all yourself.

• **Casebound**. This is the industry term for what we normally

---

Notes

"Have you ever tried to publish it yourself? I have....So now, finally, I'm the author of several books, all selling. I've cut out a little niche of the universe for myself, doing my own hoeing, reaping my own rewards...."

—Raymond Barrio
Poet, novelist.

call "hardcover". Casebound books can be quite handsome, but they are also more expensive to produce. Not ruinously expensive, but more expensive nonetheless. If money is a secondary consideration you may want to go the casebound route. On a print run of 500 books this kind of binding can add as much as two to three dollars a book to your production costs. Books containing fewer than 96 pages are normally difficult or impossible to casebind.

In addition, you will have to print a dustcover for your casebound book, and these are not cheap either. I am currently producing a casebound book for a client. The four color dustcover alone is going to run up an additional $850 in costs. For that sum of money you can bring out an entire edition of a modest paperback book.

The truth is that most poetry today is published in paperback. There is no really solid marketing reason why you should go with the hardcover option for your book. In fact, throughout all phases of publishing the distinction between hardcover and paperback is being eroded, with many top-of-the-line books now being published in paper. This has long been the tradition in Europe.

A hybrid arrangement is to do a paperback edition with stiff enough covers to hold a dustcover in place. This dresses up your paperback and gives cover flaps for sell lines, review quotes and information about the author. I have seen this technique successfully used from time to time in France, and it is apparently quite common in Japan. I have used in once, with a book of my own called *Tales of the Tobacco Country* (Era Press, 1979)

- **Paperbound**. This type of binding covers a wide range. *Perfect bound* books are like most of those that you see in a bookstore. The covers are usually printed on stiff, shiny (laminated) cover stock. The spine is squared off, and the pages fixed inside with binder's glue.

Perfectbound books vary greatly in quality. Some are very handsome, well-designed books that anyone would be proud to display on a library shelf. The Louisiana State University Press poetry series, one of the finest in the country, is perfectbound in this way. At the other end of the scale are the mass market paperbacks that you see on grocery store racks, meant to be read once or twice and thrown away.

Paperbound books may also be *saddle stitched* (stapled) along the spine. Since it normally takes a bulk of 64 or more pages to do

Notes

a decent perfect binding, books that run shorter than this are often saddle-stitched. This is certainly the most economical way to produce a book, since such a book can be brought out for a few hundred dollars.

An acquaintance of mine, the poet Mary Belle Campbell, has developed a saddle-stitched format for the titles appearing in her poetry series under the Scots Plaid Press imprint. The design of the Scots Plaid books is simple, dignified and effective.

Anyone would be pleased to be published in such a format and, indeed, some very fine poets have been. I am holding in my hand a book called *Rehearsals for Second Endings*, by Eleanor Rodman May. The cover is printed on white cover stock and bears the title, the author's name and the name and logo of the publisher. The back cover has a picture of the poet and four paragraphs of copy about the poet. Inside the cover is a flyleaf in blue bond, followed by the text itself on white bond.

The page size (trim size) is five and a half by eight and half. This is the standard size of typing and mimeograph paper. The book contains 32 pages, plus the four-page flyleaf and the cover.

Because of its standard page size a book like this one can be produced in any quick-copy shop. You could print a relatively small number in the beginning and go back for more whenever you needed them. Such a technique will help you control costs to the point that you should never have to feel that lack of funds is keeping you out of print.

More about Scots Plaid Press and similar ventures later.

How Many Do You Print?

People for whom books are important tend to overestimate the number that can be sold. You may be surprised to learn, for instance, that a first novel by an unknown author may sell fewer than 5000 copies—if that many—even when it is promoted nationwide by a major publisher with a national sales staff.

How do you estimate the number of books that you should print? Here's a case history that may help you decide. I recently published a city-county pictorial history for the town of Greenville, North Carolina. Such books are strong sells, and typically have a far greater number of potential buyers than a volume of poetry.

At the time of publication, Greenville had approximately 12,000 households. Of the 12,000 households, I reasoned, half never read anything, leaving 6000. Of this number at least half only read the newspaper, leaving 3000. Of the remaining 3000 half read

---

Notes

The secret of writing good poetry (or good anything else) is to write truly, from the very heart of yourself. This takes the greatest and most intense effort, since we all lie to ourselves constantly. Without even knowing it we assume poses and write what is expected of us rather than what is true about us.

only mass market paperbacks and no history books, leaving 1500 potential customers. Of this 1500 half might want my book but would have no money to buy it with, leaving 750. Of the 750 with both the desire and the money to read my book, a certain number would simply not get around to making the purchase. And there would always be others who—in spite of all my efforts—would never even know that the book existed.

I decided to print 500, believing that I could sell 300 immediately and the remaining 200 over a reasonable period of time. And this is precisely what happened. That was a number of years ago. I still have seven books in stock.

I would suggest—and most of those I have consulted agree with me—that an initial edition of 300 copies is entirely adequate for your purposes. If you use a quick-copy shop or a short run printer like Crane (see below), then you would do well to consider an edition as small as 100 copies. Very limited editions are possible for saddle-stitched books. For perfect bound books, the press set up and the bindery set up constitute a major portion of the cost, and this will be the same no matter how many or how few copies you print. So it doesn't work out as well for you when you want a small number of copies. | **Notes** |

Who Sets the Type?

There are two major steps in getting your book printed. It has to be typeset and it has to be printed. We'll talk more about printers later. For now let's consider the options for type.

- The printer himself may do the typesetting for you. With some printers this is an attractive option, because they keep the typesetting price low in order to get the printing job. If you go the quick-copy route, however, you will probably have to take your work in ready to print. Get a price quote from your printer and compare it with quotes you get from others who specialize in typesetting.

- You can go to a desktop publisher. These shops utilize the latest computer technology to produce completely designed pages. The quality of their type will vary with the "resolution" capabilities of their equipment. 300 dots per inch has been standard for some years, but newer equipment can produce type with a density of 400, 600, 800 and even 1000 dots per inch. I have found 300 dots per inch satisfactory, but if the higher resolution is available and affordable, specify that it be used.

• You can go to a traditional typography studio. Often these studios have desktop capabilities as well, but they are usually more expensive. They specialize in ad agency and other highly sophisticated work.

For either of these sources of type, look in the yellow pages under typesetting or typographers. Prices will vary widely from shop to shop, so always get more than one quote before deciding who will do the job.

And always be sure, when dealing with desktop publishers, to specify that you want complete page layouts, including title page, dedication, contents—everything. Their computer programs are specially designed to do this for you.

Dealing with Printers

One of the main things to remember is that there is no standard price for book production. Always get several quotes from different printers. There are local, small print shops in every town, and they are perfectly capable of bringing out a saddle-stitched book.

Perfect bound books and casebound books, however, are best handled by specialists in the field.

Price quotes from printers can vary by as much as 200% (and more) for the same job. It is very bad business indeed not to get competitive quotes and choose among them. I remember one book that was quoted to me at $5,600 by one shop. I got the book done, with exactly the same specifications, at another print shop for less than $2000.

Don't overlook the quick-copy shops or "copy centers." They are becoming more capable of handling some publishing projects every day, and they are they are usually highly competitive for very short runs. When you begin to print several hundred copies or more such shops lose their price advantage quite rapidly and become more expensive.

But most books are not printed locally at all. They are produced by specialist printers in the field who own very expensive equipment designed to do the one job of book production very well and very inexpensively. While there are many such printers available I am going to give you the names of three that I highly recommend.

Notes

"The worst thing you can do to yourself as a writer and as an artist is to allow your work to get cold, either to yourself or in terms of its time."

—*Dick Higgins*
Something Else Press

I have used both of them on many occasions and have found them to be very good and very reasonable.

The first of these shops is Bookcrafters, 140 Buchanan Street, Chelsea, Michigan, 48118-0370.

Just call them and tell them you want a quote on a printing job. Bookcrafters can also do the typesetting for you. I use Bookcrafters for most of the perfect bound books that I do that have laminated (shiny) covers and for short-run casebound books.

The second is an unbelievable shop called Crane Duplicating Service, Inc., at PO Box 437, Barnstable, Maine. Crane is quite reasonable on any very short runs and can print any number you desire, from one copy on up. I recently got 100 perfect bound, 64 page books from Crane for $160. I had already paid for the typesetting.

You have to live within the limitations of the materials Crane uses. The company loses its price advantage on longer runs, but on micro-runs they are unbeatable. Write them and tell them that you are a short run book publisher. Ask for cover samples and paper samples. They will be happy to send you these materials along with a complete price list. With this list in hand you can calculate *to the penny* the total cost of printing with Crane.

The third printer is McNaughton & Gunn, P.O. Box M2060, Ann Arbor, MI 48106. The telephone number is (313) 429-5411.

What Do Your Put On the Cover?

I can't stress enough the importance of a good, strong cover. This need not be fancy; it is better if it is not. But it should be clean and professional in appearance.

Avoid at all costs any amateur art on your cover. For some reason many poets I have known and who have consulted me on their publication projects will suggest that this or that "nice" drawing by themselves or by some relative be used as a cover. I have *never, ever* seen one of these drawings that had any professional quality to it at all. Most looked as though they would be more at home stuck on the refrigerator door. So I would suggest a general rule: no drawings on the cover.

If you do want some art on the cover go to a graphic designer as and ask for a few thumbnails for your perusal. If you see one you like strike a deal with the artist and buy what you need. Most young artists will be as anxious for a book cover credit as you are to get your book of poems out on the market. You might even be able to do a trade-off. They do the cover art. In return you do a

Notes

blurb on them that will appear on the back cover or on the verso of the title page, above the notice of copyright.

The Joys of the Jargon

Throughout this chapter I have used certain terms that you may not be familiar with—"casebound", "perfect bound", "saddle- stitched", "stock" and many others.

Like any other field the book publishing and printing business has its specialized terms and its jargon. As you get into publishing, there will be no substitute for the direct question. When confronted with a term you don't understand simply ask, "What does that mean?" Printers are kindly folk. They'll be glad to tell you. Otherwise consult the *PocketPal* I recommended in an earlier chapter.

How Much Will It Cost?

You will, of course, want to know how much all this is going to cost you. Can you afford to bring out your own book or will you be wasting your time even thinking about it?

Here are some recent examples from my own business:

- 100 copies of the 64 page book printed at Crane was $164. Typography cost another $150. Miscellaneous costs were, say, $100. Total cost for the edition: $414. The book will retail for $6.95.

- 500 copies printed with a laminated cover, perfect bound at Bookcrafters cost me $980 in 1990. This book was 48 pages long. Type cost another $200. I paid a photographer $100 for the cover shot. The book sold at retail for $9.95. Total cost for the project: $1280.

- I am currently producing 500 copies of a casebound book 164 pages long. Printing and binding are going to cost $2050. Typography (I used a desktop publisher) cost $350. The dustjacket is going to cost $650. Miscellaneous expenses will run $150. Total cost of the project: $3100. The book will retail for $18.95.

Somewhere within this range you will find a cost level suitable to your book and to your pocketbook as well. Believe me, no great

---

Notes

"...It's silly to suggest that the writing of poetry is something ethereal, a sort of soul-crashing emotional experience that wrings you. I have no fancy ideas about poetry. It doesn't come to you on the wings of a dove. It's something you work hard at."

—Louise Bogan

prestige attaches to casebound or even fancy perfectbound publication, especially since you do not expect to sell your book primarily in bookstores. The Crane or the quick copy publication works just as well for sales at readings and other special events. It is the quality of the poetry within that is going to make or break your book, so long as the overall design is done with taste and professionalism.

Allen Ginsburg's *Howl* was published by City Lights Books in San Francisco in what was virtually a plain paper edition. But its starkly black, all print cover was so appropriate to the theme that no one noticed. The book is now a highly sought-after collector's item.

Do you want to retire to the South of France and live in luxury the rest of your life? You can make a good start on it if you uncover a copy of Edgar Allen Poe's *Murders in the Rue Morgue*. This little book, printed as a paper pamphlet, is now one of the rarest and most valuable collector's items in American literature.

If your pocketbook is skinny, make a virtue out of necessity. Design a barebones book that is nevertheless very impressive. It can be done. Do it.

One caveat: You should not harbor any illusions about making a big profit on your book. I often tell this fact of life to authors that I work with and just as often they don't believe me. They say they do, but they don't. Deep down inside they all think they'll make a million. Well, let me tell you it's just not likely to happen. Even when you sell out your entire first printing, the money comes in so slowly and in such relatively small quantities that it does not feel like profit or spend like profit, even if it is profit. Poetry is published for the love of poetry. If you will follow the marketing guidelines given in this book you will make enough to cover your expenses but you are not likely to do much more than that. The fringe benefits—recognition, salary increases for teachers, income from workshops and seminars—may, of course, be more lucrative, depending on the energy with which you take advantage of them. There are many ways to profit from publication, and what you don't make in direct profits is often more than compensated for in other, far more varied ways.

The Magic Question

There is one other question that ought always to be on your lips when dealing with printers, typesetters and others from whom you will be buying goods and services. When you have made it

Notes

crystal clear what it is you want, and when you have gotten a firm quote from your supplier, then say, "Look, this is an important project to me and it is very cost sensitive. How do you think I could cut these costs down another 10 percent?"

The simple answer may be, "You can't." But very often a suggestion will be forthcoming, and it will save you money— sometimes considerable amounts of money.

Notes

Notes

Chapter 11

How To Start Your Own Small Press

When you've brought out your own book you will have learned the basics of poetry publishing. You can easily extend your activities to include publishing the work of other good poets. In so doing you will be performing a great service to the world of poetry. You will surround yourself with the poems and poets you love so well. And, taken as a whole, you may even develop a modest income for yourself.

If you decide to pursue this course great fun is in store for you. Like me, you will have become a publisher almost by default.

This is the way it happened in my case. Some years ago I was commissioned by the Bicentennial Executive Committee of Greenville, North Carolina—the town I was then living in—to write and publish a picture history of the city. At that time was a professor on the faculty of East Carolina University. I had published a couple of books with university presses but had never thought about going into the publishing business for myself. I really knew nothing about it.

But I did have this book on my hands that I had contracted to produce. I took on the whole project: research, writing, book layout, design and production. As I was designing the title page

"The reputation of the small literary press is its stock-in-trade and is built on the sheer artistic merit of the books it chooses to publish. Foundation grants and institutional subsidies depend on this reputation."

—*Thomas A. Williams,*
in How to Make
$100,000 a Year in
Desktop Publishing.

I realized that I would need the name of a publisher to put at the bottom to make things look official. I invented one—Era Press (for historical era, not the constitutional amendment)—and pasted it in place. As I looked at it I realized that I was not only a writer, I was also a publisher, at the head of my own, admittedly tiny, publishing company. And I have been publishing books ever since.

In the same way, when you choose to self-publish your own book of poems, as I recommend that you do, you have at that very moment become a publisher. You may be happy to continue in a limited role, bringing out one of your own titles from time to time. But if your personality is right for it and if you have the vim and vigor to sustain the effort it takes you might consider publishing, say, your own poetry series, broadening your scope to include the work of other poets.

Publishing is Fun

Why should you do this? For many reasons. Not the least of these is that being a publisher is a lot of fun for anyone who loves books. Your social and professional life will take a dramatic turn for the better. You will continually meet interesting people and read good poetry (and, alas, some very bad poetry). You will develop a very large circle of friends in the literary and arts communities.

You can be as aggressive or as restrained in your publishing activities as you wish to be. Given the necessary energy and interest you can become a real leader in the literary activities of your region or state. You will be one of those who make things happen. You can develop a high public visibility that will put you at the center of the kinds of activities that are meaningful to you.

The long days and years of isolation, of trying to find somebody, somewhere to talk to about poetry with will be over once and for all.

In the long run you may decide, as you learn the ropes, to publish a little magazine or works of fiction (the hardest of all to sell) and non-fiction (the easiest to market and sell).

A second very good reason to get into the publishing business is that poets need publishers—especially good ones who understand what poems are all about. With modest effort you can become one of these important *facilitators* of the art of poetry in your region.

Notes

102

You Learn As You Go

Is all this impossibly difficult? Does it not require years of training and a lengthy apprenticeship? Happily the answer to both these questions is that it clearly does not. Publishing, believe it or not, is a little like raising a family. You don't know anything at all about it when you start out but you learn very quickly as you go. Your progress can be as slow or as quick as you wish. You don't have to bring out any more titles each year than you are comfortable with.

No Financial Burden

In addition you will not have vast sums of money at risk. Remember that most books of verse can be published quite inexpensively. Since the writers themselves will participate in these costs, there will be virtually no financial pressure on you, as publisher, that you do not voluntarily assume. In addition the poets themselves will be doing most of the hands-on marketing and selling, since that's the only way that poetry will sell in any case.

How Do You Get Started?

Essentially you simply do for others what you have learned to do for yourself. The very fact that you are reading these pages and learning how to market and sell poetry means that you are more of an outgoing, take-charge person than others ,who would not be willing or able to take on such leadership responsibilities.

Those less personally skilled in such matters will need and welcome your help. They need you to design and publish their books and to teach them how to sell them—to teach them the very things that you have begun to find out about by reading and studying this book.

Your Quality Is Your Stock-in-Trade

As a literary publisher your reputation is of prime importance and must be maintained at all costs. One of the things you must do is to watch over the quality of your list of published books with great vigilance. Books will be judged, at least in part and especially by reviewers and critics, by the company they keep. Don't ac-

Notes

"Words ought to be an intense pleasure to a writer just as leather should be to a shoemaker. If there isn't that pleasure for a writer maybe he ought to be a philosopher."

—Evelyn Waugh

cept any book, even one by a close friend, that is not up to your standard. You might create an editorial review board to act as a buffer for you in accepting and rejecting manuscripts. Earlier I advised you to study a publisher's other books to see whether you thought you could entrust your work to him. You want to pass this test when others apply it to you.

Say Precisely What You Mean

One of the things you will have to do in dealing with writers is to say precisely what you mean. Most of us have had the experience—at writer's groups, say—of hiding our real opinions about poems being read to avoid hurting the feelings of some especially sensitive person.

As an editor and publisher you no longer have this luxury. You can be tactful, but speak the truth you must. When I was new in the business I often sent manuscripts back with some innocuous phrase like, "I like these but they need more work. Better luck next time". I want to tell you and I want you to understand that the hopeful poet will understand such words to mean "Polish these a bit and I'll publish them. They're great".

It's not necessary to be harsh, but if you are rejecting a collection of poems, say so: "Thank you for letting me read these. I'm afraid I can't accept them for Orpheus Press, but good luck with them elsewhere".

If you really are on the fence, be specific in your criticisms. If you want the author to make some changes or rework some poems tell him so but make it clear that he will be doing this *on speculation* and that you cannot promise to accept them once the work is done.

In these matters of editorial decision making there is absolutely no substitute for clarity.

Sign Formal Contracts

The agreement that you reach with your author will be formal, and it will be signed. It will specify all the things that you will do for the author: you will advise him in marketing and selling his book through readings and personal appearances, etc.; you will print and bind a certain number; you will send out review copies; you will compensate the author either in free copies or in a modest royalty—and so on.

You will also specify what your author will do for you. He will

Notes

pay you a subsidy of a certain amount; he will do this at a specifically appointed time; he will actively market his book (be as detailed as possible); he will warrant that he has utilized no copyrighted materials and will hold you harmless in case of litigation over copyright infringement; and so on.

You will find examples of publishing contracts in Richard Balkan's *An Author's Guide to Book Publishing* and in Judith Applebaum's *How to Get Happily Published*. These standard contracts contain far more provisions than you will need, but you can pick and choose among them.

There is an excellent short contract in publishing consultant's John Huenefeld's *Guide to Book Publishing*—highly recommended as a basic how-to guide to the entire field.

If these books and others recommended later are not in your library they can be readily obtained through an interlibrary loan request.

The Matter of Money

Publishing poetry may not cost much money but it will surely cost *something*. Where are the funds to come from? There are three sources: YOM, YPM and OPM.

- YOM stands for "your own money." You do not want to risk your own money publishing other people's poetry. Your own poetry, OK, but that of others, no. There may be some exceptions in the case of poets with very strong book-selling track records, but these will be few and far between, and I advise you in any case to look at them very carefully.

  You will be investing a good deal of time in the project anyway. And there are incidental overhead expenses. There's the telephone, the portion of the utilities you allocate to your publishing activities, random stamps and stationery, some limited travel expense—and it all adds up.

  No, get the money for actually typesetting, printing and selling the book from somewhere else. For example....

- YPM. YPM stands for "your poet's money." Expect your authors to invest in themselves just as you were advised to do in Chapter Two to get your own work published. It is quite acceptable today to get author participation in defraying these direct production expenses as well as any general overhead expenses (do not neglect to include these) that you

"A writer and nothing else: a man alone in a room with the English language, trying to get human feelings right...."

—*John K. Hutchins*

may not be able or willing to meet yourself. In return the poet gets your book editing, design and marketing skills as well as the prestige of appearing over your carefully protected and widely respected imprint.

- OPM. But there is another possibility, and that is the use of OPM, or "other people's money." No bank will lend you any money, of course, on such a hare-brained (from the traditional banking point of view) venture as that of publishing poetry, and no investors will come beating your door down for a piece of the action, either. But there are other sources, principally local and state arts councils. As you establish yourself and gain more visibility it will become more and more feasible to finance your publishing activities with grant money from such public or quasi-public agencies. Since a book of verse can be published for a few hundred dollars your demands on their resources will be not be so great as to create difficulties.

The Advantages of Not-for-Profit Status

To qualify for such funds you may have to organize your operation as a not-for-profit corporation. This does not mean that you can't get paid or earn money for your services. It just means that the corporation itself doesn't earn money and issue dividends to shareholders. Profits after expenses (including reasonable salaries) must be ploughed back into the activities defined in the corporate charter as those approved for your organization to engage in.

Businesses, industries and individuals can also be invited to contribute to non-profit corporations. Such contributions then become tax deductible. Some attorneys will contribute their services to set up such corporations when they themselves are interested in its activities. Your state arts council can also furnish guidelines as can the office of your state Secretary of State's office or the equivalent.

For More Information

Detailed instructions on setting up your own publishing company are beyond the scope of this book. Happily there are guides on the market that provide you with all the information you will need to get started, and I heartily recommend the best among them

Notes

to you.

Getting your publishing company up and going is not difficult, but you can smooth the way immensely and save great gobs of time and effort by using the resources that are available.

Here are some of the most useful. I highly recommend that you obtain them and study them. You will glean a great deal of insight into the publishing business on the micro-level, and you will gain access to a lot of hands-on, how-to information that will be exceeding valuable to you. Not to mention that for anyone interested in books and the book business, these manuals are great fun to read.

• *How to Make $100,000 a Year in Desktop Publishing,* by Thomas A. Williams. $18.95. This solid reference book tells you how to set up your business, how to get the publicity you need, how to publish poetry, magazines, journals and books. Of special interest to you will be the section on getting started in literary publishing.

• *The Self-Publishing Manual,* by Dan Poynter. This how-to book is a classic in its field and far better than any others on this topic that I have read. You will find sections on such topics as obtaining an ISBN number, establishing a marketing schedule, and getting your book and its author listed in *Books in Print* and such directories as *Contemporary Authors*. Although the book is slanted toward the publication of non-fiction, its reference material is useful to everyone starting out in the world of independent publishing.

• *Publishing Short-Run Books,* by Dan Poynter. This little book takes you through each step in the production of inexpensive books that are suitable for you poetry series. Could be worth many times its cost to you.

• *Book Marketing Made Easier,* by John Kremer. This book is a gold mine for the small publisher, containing reproducible forms for every need. Author bio and information forms, ISBN forms, Marketing schedules, consignment forms and dozens of others. They are all there. Get this book. It will same you loads of time you would otherwise waste thrashing about blindly trying to find out how to get these things done. Kremer has done the work for you.

• *Kitchen-Table Publisher,* by Thomas A. Williams. (Venture Press, available in September, 1991). *Kitchen Table Publisher*

"There is not royal road to good writing; and such paths as exist do not lead through neat critical gardens, various as they are, but through the jungles of self, the world, and of craft."

—*Jessamyn West*

tells you in detail how anyone can set up, organize and successfully run an independent publishing company from his or her own home. This book contains a step-by-step guide to setting up your company. What do you do first? What next? *Kitchen-Table Publisher* answers all these questions. An extremely valuable and useful tool. It is a complete operations manual for the small, independent publisher.

All of these titles, as well as many others of interest to the poet, novelist, non-fiction writer and self-publisher can be ordered directly from:

The Writer's Warehouse and Self-Publisher's Supply
104 South Respess Street, Washington, NC 27889

The *Writer's Warehouse* catalogue is a treasure chest of goodies and will be sent to you free of charge. Browsing through it is great fun. You may contact them by calling 919 975-2066 or by writing to the above address.

There are other books on the topic, but these are the cream of the crop. Get them and use them. You could get by without them. You could also drive a nail into a piece of wood by flailing at it with the heel of your shoe. Bt things go much more easily when you've got the right tool in your hand.

Notes

Poet's Resource Guide

Contacts and Sources

Contacts and Sources

A poet achieves success not only through the quality of his or her verse, but through networking with individuals, organizations, companies and other resource centers that can help poets and freelance writers reach their goals of successful publication. Knowing whom to call for what, knowing just who can provide you with the information or services that you need can make all the difference.

The suggestions contained in this appendix are hard-earned. They grow out of years of wrestling with the problems of marketing both my own work and that of others as writer, editor and publisher.

I built this brief resource guide by trial and error. Every entry, every idea, every contact or resource that appears on this highly selective list is there for very good reason. I have benefited from knowing about each of them, and I believe that you will, too.

Sometimes we go along for years completely unaware that the assistance, services or simple comradeship that we so badly need are readily available. We just don't know whom to call or where to write to get help we need.

Hopefully this resource guide will provide a very strong point of departure for those who read this book and who wish to thrust themselves into the mainstream of literary activity in their town, state and country.

It works for me. It works for others. It will work for you, too.

TomWilliams
Venture Press

I.
Networking Opportunities

The American poet Hart Crane, relegated to his family home in Akron, Ohio, wrote his friend Gorham Munson, back in New York, that "In this town poetry's a bedroom occupation." As a poet he felt isolated. Not only were there no other poets to exchange ideas with. He could not even find anyone who seemed interested in *talking* about poetry. The life of poetry existed only where his table and chair and pen and paper were — in his bedroom. It was a very lonely time.

Poets everywhere will experience a shock of recognition on reading Crane's description of his life in Akron. Many — maybe even most — will, at one time or another, have shared his experience of isolation. Such feelings are neither pleasant nor productive. Fortunately there is much that can be done to end our isolation and enter the literary mainstream, on a local, state and even a national level. Ready? Here are some ways to get started.

1. Join local writer's clubs and study groups and be active in them. These exist in many towns, cities and states. Generally they are open to any writer who wishes to come. To find out if a writer's club is up and running where you live check with the library, with the book editor (or the reporter who handles such assignments) on your local paper, or with the local arts council.

2. If no such club exists, fine! Start one yourself. That way you immediately assume a leadership role in the literary community. A brief article in your local newspaper will bring enough inquiries from interested writers to get things off the ground. Word of mouth will then build membership over a period of time.

3. Some writer's clubs even publish the work of their members is book form and sponsor literary competitions and prizes to stimulate submissions. Yours can do the same thing.

5. Maybe there should be *two* clubs. Literary activity covers a wide spectrum, from freelance non-fiction to short stories, from novels to poetry. These interests are not always compatible, in the sense that activities of great usefulness to one group of writers is not necessarily of interest to others. In smaller towns one is not likely to find enough writers to support a specialized club, but in the cities a poetry forum might be a desirable alternative

to an all-purpose writer's organization.

4. In addition to the local clubs there may be a state-wide organization that you should become active in. In my state the North Carolina Writer's Network is a very active group, sponsoring meetings, seminars and competitions. It acts as a very important information clearing house and provides rich networking resources for its members. In your state government there will be a department or division responsible for cultural affairs. In North Carolina this is the Department of Cultural Resources. You can contact this department, or its equivalent in your state, to get the names and addresses of state-wide organizations you should join.

The North Carolina Writer's Network is an all-purpose group catering to all writers. There is also a North Carolina Poetry Society. There may well be such a society in your state (there probably is), and you can get the name and address from your central state source, as well as from other poets. Often the poetry society will furnish information on grants, will offer literary prizes and awards and will publish, in one form or another, the work of its members.

6. You should become active in your local and state arts council or arts league. These go by various names, but they exist almost everywhere. They are active in all the arts, but you can help shape an active program for literature. Arts councils are important channels for grant money. They can, for instance, underwrite the publication of collections of poetry and other work by local writers. You can help plan such a publication and contribute to it or even become its editor.

7. Membership in these organizations is just the beginning. You will attend meetings and take a leadership role in the activities of the organization if you so desire. Always attend the business meeting portion of any yearly convocations. Speak up. Volunteer for various committee or planning work that fits your schedule of time available. Remember that all such activities build your professional image as a practising poet and enhance your chances for publication.

Action plan: Find the existing organizations for writers and join them. If none exits, start your own.

II.
Publications You Should Read.

As a member of the local and state arts councils and of the writer's clubs, societies and networks, you will begin to receive an assortment of newsletters and other materials. You should read these very carefully. They will provide a constant flow of news about new publishing opportunities, competitions and prizes, and about the availability of grant monies. These latter will be of great interest to you as you build a body of work and begin to think about book publication. This may be a source of the expense-participation money that publishers often require of poets.

There will be news of seminars, workshops and summer writer's conferences. Pay attention to these announcements. Send for more information. Even if you decide not to participate you will succeed in getting your name on another mailing list that will bring even more news and information to you, much of it quite valuable.

If you do not already do so you should subscribe to the two most important national magazines for writers, *Writer's Digest* and *The Writer*. Both are interesting in themselves and, again, will make you aware of further opportunities for networking. Judson Jerome, the current poetry columnist for *Writer's Digest* is a professional and a teacher of great skill, and you will learn much when you read his piece regularly. *The Writer* is the more laid-back and formal of the two magazines. There is a little less hype in its pages and *no* advertising from "reading services" and "publishing opportunities" of questionable merit. Its articles are very well-written, often by master writers in the field.

Both magazines are available on newsstands. My advice is to buy a copy and take advantage of the reduced rate subscription card that is included in almost every issue. Or you may write directly to:

Writer's Digest
1507 Dana Avenue
Cincinnati, OH (45207
(513) 531-2222

The Writer
120 Boylston Street
Boston MA 02116

III.
Books You Should Own

One could draw up a virtually unlimited list of books that any serious writer should own. There are, however, a basic few — in addition to your dictionary and thesaurus — that you will consult time and again. You will consult them, that is, if they are available on your bookshelf and ready to hand. Here are a few of the most important among them.

1. *Literary Market Place.* (R.R.Bowker). This book is usually referred to by its initials:

LMP. This great reference volume is the bible of the book publishing business. If you need a contact in any area of book publishing and marketing you can find the names and addresses you need in LMP. Like most reference books LMP is expensive, but it is worth every penny of its price. Of course, if you are a frequent library-goer or if you live across the street from the library, you can use the one that is probably in the reference room. My experience, though, is that I seldom used to consult LMP at the library, even though I needed to. Since I have owned my own copy I find that I use it constantly.

LMP is chock full of information that can be very valuable to you. You might browse through the lengthy list of "Literary and Writer's Associations" and write to those that interest you. Though not complete it contains many listings for organizations as diverse as "The Poetry Society of America", "Poets and Writers, Inc.", the "Jane Austin Society" and the "Mystery Writers of America."

LMP is not on sale in bookstores and must be ordered directly from R.R. Bowker. It is quite expensive, costing nearly $100. The toll-free number is 1-800-521 8110. Or you may write:

R.R. Bowker,
Order Dept.
PO Box 762,
New York, NY 10011.

2. *Writer's Market* and *Poet's Market* (Writer's Digest Books). These books, published and updated annually, contain listings for many of the major markets for poetry.

The listings give, usually, the name of the editor to whom poems should be submitted, payment policies and terms, and addresses. While they are far from complete (see below) they are the very best place to start on your search for publishing opportunities.

You will miss, in spite of yourself, many a chance if you do not have these books on hand. Human nature being what it is — and judging by my own share of it — you will be delayed for weeks at a time in getting your poem packs back out to new publications for consideration merely because you do not have the proper address on hand to send it to.

Both *Writer's Market* and *Poet's Market* can be bought in most well-stocked bookstores. They are, happily, quite affordable.

2. *All-in-One Directory*. (Gebbie Press). For the many — the *very* many — markets that may not be covered in the two Writer's Digest titles discussed above, consult this book. It contains listings for house magazines and many other periodicals that might otherwise escape your notice. Complete editorial and address material is given. The address of

Gebbie Press is as follows:

Gebbie Press
PO Box 1000
New Paltz, New York, 12561-0017
(914) 255-7560

Alternatively, you may consult *Working Press of the Nation*, a five volume reference work, in your library.

3. *The International Directory of Small Magazines and Literary Presses*. (Dustbooks). This directory is of special interest to those involved in wholly literary writing (as distinct from commercial writing), as many poets are. It lists hundreds of small presses and literary reviews which could be interested in your verse. This book can be ordered by most bookstores, and it may be on the shelves of the larger ones, especially the shelves of university bookstores. Or, it may be ordered directly from Dustbooks. The address (which I just looked up in the LMP on my office shelf) is as follows:

Dustbooks
PO Box 100
Paradise, CA 95969.
(916) 877-6110

IV.
Getting Printed.

In *How to Publish Your Poetry* I recommend without hesitation that you consider organizing a personal publishing company and bringing out your own book. I suggest some printers and strategies for producing your book at an affordable price. One of these sources, Crane Duplicating, is so unusual that it deserves fuller treatment. It is unusual in that this company can print as few as ten, fifty or a hundred books at a very affordable price. Thus you can get your book out and test the market quickly and easily.

In dealing with Crane bear in mind (a) that if you don't like their cover stock you can furnish your own; (b) that in any case you will furnish the cover design; and (c) that you must make clear to them that you will be placing your book on sale and that it is not merely a bound galley (otherwise they may print the words "bound galley" on the cover, and you do not want that).

Turnaround time is very fast. Books can be shipped out to you a week to ten days after your camera-ready copy is received in the Crane office. I am enclosing a Crane price list that is current as of the winter of 90-91. Write to Crane for a full information kit and samples of cover and body stock, along with a current price list. Remember that for longer print runs you will usually do better with a standard book printer.

V.
Some Forms That You Will Need

The following membership applications and forms are furnished to you to facilitate your work. They may be duplicated on a photo-copier, filled out and sent in. The forms include the following:

1. *Copyright* forms necessary for securing a copyright on your published or unpublished work, along with an explanation of the copyright application process. Please note that whereas the form included here states that the sum of $10 should be sent in with your application, the correct fee is now $20.

2. A Library of Congress form for obtaining a Library of Congress catalogue number and for securing cataloging in publication data.

3. Information that will nable you to include your name in *Contemporary Authors*, a standard "who's who" directory included in most library collections.

4. Information on COSMEP, one of the leading organizations for writers and independent pubilshers. If you like the sample newsletter, go ahead and join. It could be very valuable to you to do so.

5. A catalogue of other books of interest to writers and independent publishers. Any of these books may be ordered from the Writer's Warehouse and Self-Publisher's Supply, 104 South Respess Street, Washington, NC 27889

Contemporary Authors

A BIO BIBLIOGRAPHICAL GUIDE TO CURRENT WRITERS IN FICTION, GENERAL NONFICTION, POETRY, JOURNALISM, DRAMA, MOTION PICTURES, TELEVISION, AND OTHER FIELDS

Dear Author:

You are cordially invited to complete the enclosed questionnaire and return it to us as soon as possible so that your bio-bibliographical sketch can be included in the next volume of CONTEMPORARY AUTHORS.

In case you are not already familiar with CA (published since 1962 and now widely used in thousands of libraries and editorial offices around the world), I am enclosing a brochure which describes the series and gives examples of sketches based on questionnaires completed by other authors.

If you will fill in the enclosed personal information form and return it promptly, we will prepare a manuscript of your proposed listing for your approval. If you have a succinct resume which gives most of the requested information, simply attach the resume to the form and fill in only those parts of the CA form not covered in your prepared material.

Of course, there is <u>never</u> an obligation or charge for a listing in CONTEMPORARY AUTHORS. For an objective appraisal of our work, you may wish to contact your local library. If you require additional information, do not hesitate to contact me.

Cordially,

Jane A. Bowden
Editor

Write to the above address
for an author imofrmation
form.

GALE RESEARCH COMPANY   •   BOOK TOWER   •   DETROIT, MICHIGAN 48226

COSMEP
The International Association of Independent Publishers

P.O. Box 703
San Francisco, CA 94101
(415) 922-9490

Special offer: join now for 1990 at the usual $50.00 rate, and we'll throw in the rest of 1989 FREE.

Dear Publisher,

We would like to invite you to join COSMEP, the world's oldest and largest trade association for small publishers.

Founded as a non-profit organization in 1968, COSMEP has members in all fifty states, and in eleven foreign countries. Its members publish books and magazines in all genres, and range in size from one-book publishers to medium-sized trade houses that bring out dozens of titles per year.

Membership is open to any press or periodical. Self-publishers may join, as may presses or publications still in the planning stage. Suppliers and others allied to the trade may join as associate members.

Membership (regular or associate) is only $50.00 per year.

A subscription to the COSMEP Newsletter is included with either kind of membership. The Newsletter does not accept advertising. We concentrate, instead, on providing members with the most up-to-date and reliable information available, and on printing articles and column by some of the leading people in the publishing field.

COSMEP holds an annual publishers' conference that consists of three days of intensive marketing seminars. The conference will be held in Chicago in 1989, in San Francisco in 1990, and in Boston in 1991.

COSMEP exhibits members' publications at the annual conventions of the American Booksellers Association and the American Library Associati We rent mailing lists at bargain prices, and provide advice on any publishing problems that members may encounter. And of course we also function as a trade association representing the interests of the independent publisher.

Yet other services are available through COSMEP's association membership in Support Services Alliance (SSA). These include Blue Shield insurance at group rates, credit reports and collections, a travel service and discounts of various kinds.

To join COSMEP, just mail a check for $50.00 to the above address. We try to keep bureaucracy to a minimum and thus don't require the filling out of application forms. But do indicate the name under which membership should be entered. Normally, this will be a press name, but the name of an individual is fine too. Payment should be made in U.S. dollars, and overseas publishers should add $10.00 if they wish newsletters sent airmail.

Cordially,

Richard Morris
Executive Director

> Write to COSMEP
> for a membership application
> form and further information.

Board of Directors: John B. McHugh, Chair • Henry Berry, Secretary • Mark Nolan, Treasurer
Marilyn Ross • John Kremer • **Executive Director:** Richard Morris

HOW TO FILL OUT FORM TX

Specific Instructions for Spaces 1-4

> - The line-by-line instructions on this page are keyed to the spaces on the first page of Form TX, printed opposite.
> - Please read through these instructions before you start filling out your application, and refer to the specific instructions for each space as you go along.

SPACE 1: TITLE

- **Title of this Work:** Every work submitted for copyright registration must be given a title that is capable of identifying that particular work. If the copies or phonorecords of the work bear a title (or an identifying phrase that could serve as a title), transcribe its wording completely and exactly on the application. Remember that indexing of the registration and future identification of the work will depend on the information you give here.

- **Periodical or Serial Issue:** Periodicals and other serials are publications issued at intervals under a general title, such as newspapers, magazines, journals, newsletters, and annuals. If the work being registered is an entire issue of a periodical or serial, give the over-all title of the periodical or serial in the space headed "Title of this Work," and add the specific information about the issue in the spaces provided. If the work being registered is a contribution to a periodical or serial issue, follow the instructions for "Publication as a Contribution."

- **Previous or Alternative Titles:** Complete this space if there are any additional titles for the work under which someone searching for the registration might be likely to look, or under which a document pertaining to the work might be recorded.

- **Publication as a Contribution:** If the work being registered has been published as a contribution to a periodical, serial, or collection, give the title of the contribution in the space headed "Title of this Work." Then, in the line headed "Publication as a Contribution," give information about the larger work in which the contribution appeared.

SPACE 2: AUTHORS

- **General Instructions:** First decide, after reading these instructions, who are the "authors" of this work for copyright purposes. Then, unless the work is a "collective work" (see below), give the requested information about every "author" who contributed any appreciable amount of copyrightable matter to this version of the work. If you need further space, use the attached Continuation Sheet and, if necessary, request additional Continuation Sheets (Form TX/Con).

- **Who is the "Author"?** Unless the work was "made for hire," the individual who actually created the work is its "author." In the case of a work made for hire, the statute provides that "the employer or other person for whom the work was prepared is considered the author."

- **What is a "Work Made for Hire"?** A "work made for hire" is defined as: (1) "a work prepared by an employee within the scope of his or her employment"; or (2) "a work specially ordered or commissioned" for certain uses specified in the statute, but only if there is a written agreement to consider it a "work made for hire."

- **Collective Work:** In the case of a collective work, such as a periodical issue, anthology, collection of essays, or encyclopedia, it is sufficient to give information about the author of the collective work as a whole.

- **Author's Identity Not Revealed:** If an author's contribution is "anonymous" or "pseudonymous," it is not necessary to give the name and dates for that author. However, the citizenship and domicile of the author **must** be given in all cases, and information about the nature of that author's contribution to the work should be included if possible.

- **Name of Author:** The fullest form of the author's name should be given. If you have checked "Yes" to indicate that the work was "made for hire," give the full legal name of the employer (or other person for whom the work was prepared). You may also include the name of the employee (for example, "Elster Publishing Co., employer for hire of John Ferguson"). If the work is "anonymous" you may: (1) leave the line blank, or (2) state "Anonymous" in the line, or (3) reveal the author's identity. If the work is "pseudonymous" you may (1) leave the line blank, or (2) give the pseudonym and identify it as such (for example: "Huntley Haverstock, pseudonym"), or (3) reveal the author's name, making clear which is the real name and which is the pseudonym (for example, "Judith Barton, whose pseudonym is Madeleine Elster").

- **Dates of Birth and Death:** If the author is dead, the statute requires that the year of death be included in the application unless the work is anonymous or pseudonymous. The author's birth date is optional, but is useful as a form of identification. Leave this space blank if the author's contribution was a "work made for hire."

- **"Anonymous" or "Pseudonymous" Work:** An author's contribution to a work is "anonymous" if that author is not identified on the copies or phonorecords of the work. An author's contribution to a work is "pseudonymous" if that author is identified on the copies or phonorecords under a fictitious name.

- **Author's Nationality or Domicile:** Give the country of which the author is a citizen, or the country in which the author is domiciled. The statute requires that either nationality or domicile be given in all cases.

- **Nature of Authorship:** After the words "Author of" give a brief general statement of the nature of this particular author's contribution to the work. Examples: "Entire text"; "Co-author of entire text"; "Chapters 11-14"; "Editorial revisions"; "Compilation and English translation"; "Illustrations."

SPACE 3: CREATION AND PUBLICATION

- **General Instructions:** Do not confuse "creation" with "publication." Every application for copyright registration must state "the year in which creation of the work was completed." Give the date and nation of first publication only if the work has been published.

- **Creation:** Under the statute, a work is "created" when it is fixed in a copy or phonorecord for the first time. Where a work has been prepared over a period of time, the part of the work existing in fixed form on a particular date constitutes the created work on that date. The date you give here should be the year in which the author completed the particular version for which registration is now being sought, even if other versions exist or if further changes or additions are planned.

- **Publication:** The statute defines "publication" as "the distribution of copies or phonorecords of a work to the public by sale or other transfer of ownership, or by rental, lease, or lending"; a work is also "published" if there has been an "offering to distribute copies or phonorecords to a group of persons for purposes of further distribution, public performance, or public display." Give the full date (month, day, year) when, and the country where, publication first occurred. If first publication took place simultaneously in the United States and other countries, it is sufficient to state "U.S.A."

SPACE 4: CLAIMANT(S)

- **Name(s) and Address(es) of Copyright Claimant(s):** Give the name(s) address(es) of the copyright claimant(s) in this work. The statute provides that copyright in a work belongs initially to the author of the work (including, in the case of a work made for hire, the employer or other person for whom the work was prepared). The copyright claimant is either the author of the work or a person or organization that has obtained ownership of the copyright initially belonging to the author.

- **Transfer:** The statute provides that, if the copyright claimant is not the author, the application for registration must contain "a brief statement of how the claimant obtained ownership of the copyright." If any copyright claimant named in space 4 is not an author named in space 2, give a brief, general statement summarizing the means by which that claimant obtained ownership of the copyright.

FORM TX

UNITED STATES COPYRIGHT OFFICE

REGISTRATION NUMBER

TX	TXU

EFFECTIVE DATE OF REGISTRATION

....
Month   Day   Year

DO NOT WRITE ABOVE THIS LINE. IF YOU NEED MORE SPACE, USE CONTINUATION SHEET

① Title

TITLE OF THIS WORK:

PREVIOUS OR ALTERNATIVE TITLES:

If a periodical or serial give: Vol....... No....... Issue Date ....

PUBLICATION AS A CONTRIBUTION: (If this work was published as a contribution to a periodical, serial, or collection, give information about the collective work in which the contribution appeared.)

Title of Collective Work: .... Vol....... No....... Date .... Pages..............

② Author(s)

IMPORTANT: Under the law, the "author" of a "work made for hire" is generally the employer, not the employee (see instructions). If any part of this work was "made for hire" check "Yes" in the space provided, give the employer (or other person for whom the work was prepared) as "Author" of that part, and leave the space for dates blank.

1

NAME OF AUTHOR:

Was this author's contribution to the work a "work made for hire"?   Yes...... No......

DATES OF BIRTH AND DEATH:
Born .... Died ....
(Year)   (Year)

AUTHOR'S NATIONALITY OR DOMICILE:
Citizen of .... } or { Domiciled in ....
(Name of Country)   (Name of Country)

AUTHOR OF: (Briefly describe nature of this author's contribution)

WAS THIS AUTHOR'S CONTRIBUTION TO THE WORK:
Anonymous? Yes...... No......
Pseudonymous? Yes...... No......
If the answer to either of these questions is "Yes, see detailed instructions attached.

2

NAME OF AUTHOR:

Was this author's contribution to the work a "work made for hire"?   Yes...... No......

DATES OF BIRTH AND DEATH:
Born .... Died ....
(Year)   (Year)

AUTHOR'S NATIONALITY OR DOMICILE:
Citizen of .... } or { Domiciled in ....
(Name of Country)   (Name of Country)

AUTHOR OF: (Briefly describe nature of this author's contribution)

WAS THIS AUTHOR'S CONTRIBUTION TO THE WORK:
Anonymous? Yes...... No......
Pseudonymous? Yes...... No......
If the answer to either of these questions is "Yes, see detailed instructions attached.

3

NAME OF AUTHOR:

Was this author's contribution to the work a "work made for hire"?   Yes...... No......

DATES OF BIRTH AND DEATH:
Born .... Died ....
(Year)   (Year)

AUTHOR'S NATIONALITY OR DOMICILE:
Citizen of .... } or { Domiciled in ....
(Name of Country)   (Name of Country)

AUTHOR OF: (Briefly describe nature of this author's contribution)

WAS THIS AUTHOR'S CONTRIBUTION TO THE WORK:
Anonymous? Yes...... No......
Pseudonymous? Yes...... No......
If the answer to either of these questions is "Yes, see detailed instructions attached.

③ Creation and Publication

YEAR IN WHICH CREATION OF THIS WORK WAS COMPLETED:

Year...........

(This information must be given in all cases.)

DATE AND NATION OF FIRST PUBLICATION:

Date.........................
(Month)   (Day)   (Year)

Nation.........................
(Name of Country)

(Complete this block ONLY if this work has been published.)

④ Claimant(s)

NAME(S) AND ADDRESS(ES) OF COPYRIGHT CLAIMANT(S):

TRANSFER: (If the copyright claimant(s) named here in space 4 are different from the author(s) named in space 2, give a brief statement of how the claimant(s) obtained ownership of the copyright.)

- *Complete all applicable spaces (numbers 5-11) on the reverse side of this page*
- *Follow detailed instructions attached*
- *Sign the form at line 10*

DO NOT WRITE HERE

Page 1 of .... pages

DO NOT WRITE ABOVE THIS LINE. IF YOU NEED ADDITIONAL SPACE, USE CONTINUATION SHEET (FORM TX/CON)

PREVIOUS REGISTRATION:

- Has registration for this work, or for an earlier version of this work, already been made in the Copyright Office?   Yes . . . . No . . . .
- If your answer is "Yes," why is another registration being sought? (Check appropriate box)
  - ☐ This is the first published edition of a work previously registered in unpublished form.
  - ☐ This is the first application submitted by this author as copyright claimant.
  - ☐ This is a changed version of the work. as shown by line 6 of this application.
- If your answer is "Yes," give: Previous Registration Number . . . . Year of Registration . . . .

5 Previous Registration

COMPILATION OR DERIVATIVE WORK: (See instructions)

PREEXISTING MATERIAL: (Identify any preexisting work or works that this work is based on or incorporates.)

. . . .

MATERIAL ADDED TO THIS WORK: (Give a brief. general statement of the material that has been added to this work and in which copyright is claimed.)

. . . .

6 Compilation or Derivative Work

MANUFACTURERS AND LOCATIONS: (If this is a published work consisting preponderantly of nondramatic literary material in English. the law may require that the copies be manufactured in the United States or Canada for full protection. If so, the names of the manufacturers who performed certain processes, and the places where these processes were performed *must* be given. See instructions for details.)

NAMES OF MANUFACTURERS	PLACES OF MANUFACTURE
. . . .	. . . .
. . . .	. . . .
. . . .	. . . .

7 Manufacturing

REPRODUCTION FOR USE OF BLIND OR PHYSICALLY-HANDICAPPED PERSONS: (See instructions)

- Signature of this form at space 10. and a check in one of the boxes here in space 8. constitutes a non-exclusive grant of permission to the Library of Congress to reproduce and distribute solely for the blind and physically handicapped and under the conditions and limitations prescribed by the regulations of the Copyright Office: (1) copies of the work identified in space 1 of this application in Braille (or similar tactile symbols); or (2) phonorecords embodying a fixation of a reading of that work; or (3) both.

  a ☐ Copies and phonorecords   b ☐ Copies Only   c ☐ Phonorecords Only

8 License For Handicapped

DEPOSIT ACCOUNT: (If the registration fee is to be charged to a Deposit Account established in the Copyright Office. give name and number of Account.)

Name: . . . .

Account Number: . . . .

CORRESPONDENCE: (Give name and address to which correspondence about this application should be sent.)

Name: . . . .

Address: . . . . (Apt.)

. . . .
(City)   (State)   (ZIP)

9 Fee and Correspondence

CERTIFICATION: ✱ I, the undersigned. hereby certify that I am the: (Check one)

☐ author ☐ other copyright claimant ☐ owner of exclusive right(s) ☐ authorized agent of: . . . .
(Name of author or other copyright claimant. or owner of exclusive right(s))

of the work identified in this application and that the statements made by me in this application are correct to the best of my knowledge.

Handwritten signature: (X) . . . .

Typed or printed name. . . . . Date . . . .

10 Certification (Application must be signed)

MAIL CERTIFICATE TO	
. . . . (Name)	
. . . . (Number, Street and Apartment Number)	(Certificate will be mailed in window envelope)
. . . . (City) (State) (ZIP code)	

11 Address - For Return of Certificate

✱ 17 U.S.C. § 506(e): Any person who knowingly makes a false representation of a material fact in the application for copyright registration provided for by section 409. or in any written statement filed in connection with the application. shall be fined not more than $2.500.

REQUEST FOR PREASSIGNMENT OF LIBRARY OF CONGRESS CATALOG CARD NUMBER

NOTE: Card numbers cannot be preassigned to books which are already published.

DATE: _____

PUBLISHER'S NAME ON TITLE PAGE: _____

YOUR NAME: _____ PHONE NUMBER: _____

Type or print clearly the complete address to which the preassigned card number should be sent. (This will be your return mailing label.)

FOR CIP OFFICE USE

Library of Congress Catalog
Card Number preassigned is:

Transcribe the information in items 1-8 exactly in the form and order in which it will appear on the title or copyright pages of the printed book. Use only those abbreviations which will actually appear on these pages. **(Please attach a copy of the proposed title page, if available)**

1. Author(s) _____

2. Editor(s) _____

3. Title _____

4. Subtitle _____

5. Edition (exactly as printed in the publication, e.g. second edition, revised edition, etc.) _____

6. U.S. place of publication: City _____ State _____

7. Any copublisher(s) and place _____

8. Series title and numbering, exactly as printed in the publication _____

9. Approximate number of pages _____ 10. Number of volumes _____ 11. ISBN _____

12. Binding: ☐ Hardcover ☐ Paperback 13. Proposed date of publication: Month _____ Year _____

14. Does (or will) the title in item 3 appear at periodic intervals, e.g. annually, quarterly, etc.? ☐ Yes ☐ No

15. Will this publication be submitted later for CIP data? ☐ Yes ☐ No 16. Language of text, if other than English _____

For each title which is preassigned a Library of Congress catalog card number, the Library of Congress requires one non-returnable complimentary copy of the best edition of the published book. If selected for the Library's collections, the book will be cataloged. A postage-free, self-addressed label will be sent with the preassigned card number for your convenience in mailing the required advance copy of the work as soon as printed. This copy is in addition to copyright deposit copies.

Send this form to: **Library of Congress
Cataloging in Publication Division
Washington, DC 20540**

FOR CIP OFFICE USE ONLY. DO NOT WRITE BELOW THIS LINE

Searching notes:

☐ Write to the Library of Congress
for thier freeinformation booklet
on the LC cataloguing process.

RECD: _____

ASGN: _____

SENT: _____

APIF : _____

607-7 (rev 10/86)

This is a BOUND GALLEY PRICE LIST only. Finished Books are priced separately. Bound Galley Prices include: Plates, Textpaper: 50# Hammermill South Shore Vellum White, Offset printing, Black ink.

Cover stock: 65# Hammermill Cover Antique White or Colored. Printed in Black ink FC, Spine and BC. Perfect bound. Carton packed. Shipping at cost. For more information call: Kenyon Gregoire or Geoffrey Mawby.

Crane Duplicating Service, Inc. · P.O. Box 487 · Barnstable, MA 02630 · 508-362-3441

PRICE LIST

FOR BOOKS UP TO 5⅜ × 8¼

Sets	Cost per Page	Sets	Cost per Page	Sets	Cost per Page
20	.0488	45	.0298	150	.0188
21	.0478	46	.0295	155	.0186
22	.0467	47	.0291	160	.0185
23	.0456	48	.0287	165	.0183
24	.0446	49	.0284	170	.0181
25	.0435	50	.0279	175	.0179
26	.0427	55	.0272	180	.0178
27	.0418	60	.0265	185	.0177
28	.0411	65	.0257	190	.0175
29	.0402	70	.0249	195	.0173
30	.0394	75	.0242	200	.0172
31	.0385	80	.0234	250	.0163
32	.0376	85	.0226	300	.0155
33	.0368	90	.0219	350	.0147
34	.0359	95	.0211	400	.0138
35	.0351	100	.0204	450	.0129
36	.0345	105	.0202	500	.0121
37	.0340	110	.0201	600	.0112
38	.0335	115	.0199	700	.0103
39	.0330	120	.0197	800	.0094
40	.0325	125	.0196	900	.0085
41	.0319	130	.0194	1000	.0076
42	.0314	135	.0193	1500	.0074
43	.0309	140	.0191	2000	.0072
44	.0304	145	.0189		

EXTRAS available at additional costs: Page make-up, Text reductions or enlargements, Halftone screening, 50# or 60# Cream White text stock, CIS - Coated one side cover stock, Colored inks, Saddlewire, Spiral bound, Inserts, Shrink wrap, Oblong and Finished books.

FOR BOOKS 6 × 9 TO 8¼ × 10⅝

Sets	Cost per Page	Sets	Cost per Page	Sets	Cost per Page
20	.0976	45	.0596	150	.0376
21	.0956	46	.0590	155	.0372
22	.0934	47	.0582	160	.0370
23	.0912	48	.0574	165	.0366
24	.0892	49	.0568	170	.0362
25	.0870	50	.0558	175	.0358
26	.0854	55	.0544	180	.0356
27	.0836	60	.0530	185	.0354
28	.0822	65	.0514	190	.0350
29	.0804	70	.0498	195	.0346
30	.0788	75	.0484	200	.0344
31	.0770	80	.0468	250	.0326
32	.0752	85	.0452	300	.0310
33	.0736	90	.0438	350	.0294
34	.0718	95	.0422	400	.0276
35	.0702	100	.0408	450	.0258
36	.0690	105	.0404	500	.0242
37	.0680	110	.0402	600	.0224
38	.0670	115	.0398	700	.0206
39	.0660	120	.0394	800	.0188
40	.0650	125	.0392	900	.0170
41	.0638	130	.0388	1000	.0152
42	.0628	135	.0386	1500	.0148
43	.0618	140	.0382	2000	.0144
44	.0608	145	.0378		

Example of Price List usage: 60 copies of a 250 page, 5⅜ × 8¼ book, 250 pages × .0265 per page, equals $6.625 per copy × 60 copies = $397.50.

Other Best-Selling Resource Guides

1019 Beginner's Mistakes You Must Avoid
by Thomas A. Williams

This is the real skinny on a matter of great importance to anyone starting out as a freelancer. You can learn these things the hard way, via a few years of trial and error and mountains of rejection slips. Or you can read this special press report from an editor with long experience who will reveal to you precisely what you need to know. Many of the items on his list will be things you never dreamed of. Editors are looking for writers who will produce solid, publishable copy. They will shy away at the first sing that a new writer is, in fact, a beginner in the field—especially in the better paying markets that you wan to break in to. Learn how to keep your beginner status to yourself. What your editor doesn't know won't hurt him or her—and can be a great boost to you.

Venture Press. Ringbound. $8.95

1020 Freelancer's Indispensable Start-up Kit
by Thomas A. Williams

Contains six venture press books, plus *How to Make $100,000 a Year in Desktop Publishing*. Includes *The Query Letter that Never Fails, The Article Format That Always Sells, How to Publish Your Poetry, Ten Books You Can Write and Publish for Pleasure and for Profit*, and *Tom Williams' Self-Publisher's Handbook*. Also contains invaluable forms to organize your writing life that keep you profitable and productive. Successful writers know that organization of effort is fundamental in the quest for publication. These forms alone, if conscientiously utilized, can transform your writing life.

Venture Press. Ringbound. An $119 value, just $79.95

1021 How to Write a Living Family History
by Thomas A. Williams

On assignment for others or just for yourself, you can write a living family history quickly and well by using the techniques outlined in this book. No experience needed. Drawing heavily on oral history methods, and the collection of documents, photographs, clippings, scrapbooks and other memorabilia, these book bind generations together and become treasured heirlooms. Method makes project suitable for beginning as well as experienced writers. Contains worksheets and planning guide.

Venture Press. Ringbound. $24.95

149MBP   Mont Blanc Diplomat Pen

Enjoy the pleasure of writing with the world's finest pen. The extraordinary Mont Blanc Diplomat has a 14 karat nib with platinum coating, 14 karat gold-plated trim. Black. Piston filling. Recommended retail, $295.00

Writer's Warehouse price, just $250.00.
144MBP Black
144RMBP Burgundy

Slender Mont Blanc series in black or burgundy for those who desire a smaller pen that the traditional Diplomat while maintaining superb Mont Blanc quality. Suggested retail $180. Please specify color when ordering.

Writer's Warehouse price, just $160.00

2011 The Self-Publishing Manual: How to Write, Print and Publish Your Own Book. by Dan Poynter. A classic in its field, Poynter's book is acknowledged as one of the most authoritative guides on writing, publishing, promoting, marketing and distributing books. Judith Applebaum, author of "How to Get Happily Published" calls this book "The best self-publishing manual on the market.

5th revised edition. Softcover. $19.95

2022 How to Make A Whole Lot More Than $1,000,000 Writing, Commissioning, Publishing and Selling "How-to" Information. by Dr. Jeffrey Lant.

This book is one of the most valuable on the market for the person who whats to generate and sell "how-to" information. It is absolutely chock-full of money-making ideas. The chapter on market-oriented thinking (as contrasted with product-centered thinking) is alone worth the cover price of $35.00. Lant prides himself on giving all the information needed to get a project underway, keep it going, and make money from it. He has succeeded. This big (552 pages) is the one want if you're serious about making big money from books, booklets audio cassettes and special reports that you develop and sell on your own. Powerful stuff.

JLA Publications. Paperbound. $35.00

For Immediate Shipment, Call (919) 975-2066

Writer's Warehouse & Self-Publisher's Supply
104 South Respess Street
Washington, NC 27889
(919) 975-2066

Other Best-Selling Resource Guides

1014 How to Publish Your Poetry: The First Ever Marketing Manual and Success Guide for Poets.
by Thomas A. Williams

This is the book many poets have been waiting for. The perennial problem of getting your poetry published will be solved when you follow the methods detailed in this great, new book. Now, you don't have to sit back and wait. You can shake free of "editor's reluctance" and join the ranks of published poets. Tried-and-true strategies that lead to publication, readings, grants. Step-by-step rules for implementation include such topics as the following:

- How, by using this intensive marketing system you can publish your poetry.
- What every poet must know about the economics of publishing: the dollars and cents of publication. A very valuable insight into the economic world in which publishers live and make their decisions.
- The seven secret ingredients of poems that editors will want to buy.
- How to publish your poems in magazines. A proven marketing method selling to magazines. Use it and you will see your poems in print.
- How to find a publisher for your book of poetry: how to package your poetry and yourself to enhance your chances for success.
- The unabashed poets guide to publicity and self-promotion. These basic marketing and self-promotion techniques will build your reputation as a writer and result in more frequent and more successful publication.
- The pleasures of signing and selling. Autograph parties are your first-line marketing events and will result in your first substantial sales—*if* you plan them for maximum impact.
- How to give great poetry readings. Most books of verse that are sold are sold at readings. You learn how to give readings that work, how to use showbiz techniques to highlight your poetry and sell your books.
- How to publish it yourself. The big news is that self-publication has become very respectable and is being practices by more and more important writers. You learn how you can publish, market and profit from your own book of poetry.
- How to design and print a book. All the details you will need on designing and printing your own book.
- How to start your own small press. Once you publish your own book you may as well publish the books of other poets, too! Learn how to become an important part of the literary community in your state and region.

Venture Press. Ringbound. $24.95

1015 Ten Books You Can Write and Publish for Pleasure and Profit by Thomas A. Williams

This book reveals a tested, sure-fire formula for successful independent publishing. Includes details of ten fail-proof book ideas that follow this formula. Perfect for beginners or busy professionals, since writing and research are easily done. This is the way I got started in publishing. I have personally carried out each of these ideas and can vouch for their success. You can do the same thing. For novice and experienced writers who want to move up a notch and publish their own work.

Venture Press. Ringbound for easy reference. $16.95

1016 Tom Williams' Self-Publisher's Handbook

If you are considering self publication read this first. This succinct book gives you all the details at a glance. It tells you in no-nonsense language what you need to know: sales you can expect, how much to charge, difficulties to avoid, how to get free publicity in print and on TV, plus a three point, tried-and- true success formula. This last alone is worth the price of the book.

Venture Press. Ringbound for easy reference. $12.95

1017 How to Save (Lots of) Money Printing Your Books, Magazines and Booklets by Thomas A. Williams

You can save thousands of dollars printing your books, magazines and booklets when you utilize the tips in this book. I learned this through many years of trial and error. Now I get much better printing for a fraction of what I used to pay. You can too. Tells why you pay too much when you go to your local printer, specialty printers you need and how to find them, three essential questions you *must* ask if you want to get a lower price, how to get and compare printing quotes. If you are a publisher, self-publisher or editor of a magazine or newsletter, this book means money in the bank—*your* bank.

Venture Press. Ringbound. $19.95

1018 How to Start Your Own Small Press
by Thomas A. Williams

You can become a recognized literary publisher with your own small press and reap the financial and professional rewards that flow from it. It is simple and affordable when you implement the rules and strategies contained in this book. This book tells you— and detailed, step-by-step instructions—how to make your dream a reality and join the book world at the head of your own publishing company. Financing sources, too. How to get grants. Info works for cooperatives, writer's clubs, arts councils and other organizations as well as for individuals.
Venture Press. Ringbound. $29.95

For Immediate Shipment, Call (919) 975-2066

Writer's Warehouse & Self-Publisher's Supply
104 South Respess Street
Washington, NC 27889
(919) 975-2066

Other Best-Selling Resource Guides

1021 How to Make $100,000 a Year in Desktop Publishing
by Thomas A. Williams.

This fabulous new book tells how anyone can make $100,000 or more a year in a home-based business utilizing his or her own system. The author set up shop in 1986 with one Mac Plus and a laser printer. Since then he has published highly profitable books, magazines, travel guides, real estate directories. apartment guides and other publications. *How to make $100,000 a Year in Desktop Publishing* tells in clear, precise language how others can do this too. *Desktop Publisher* gives complete, step-by-step instructions on such topics as:

- How to Publish a Quality of Life Magazine
- How to Publish a Weekly Newspaper or Shopper
- How to Publish a Travel and Tourism Guide
- How to Publish a Newcomer's Guide
- How to Publish a City Magazine
- How to Sell Information by Mail
- How to Make Money Publishing Literary Books
- How to Publish a City or County History
- How to Get Better Printing for Far Less Money
- How to Set Up and Organize Your New Publishing Company
- Secrets of Big Profits in Inexpensive Tabloid Publications.
- How to Make Money Publishing Family Histories.
- How to Publish an Association Membership Directory.

Betterway Publications. $19.95

1022. The Query Letter That Never Fails
by Thomas A. Williams

Why do others get published when you don't? Learn the essential elements that make query letters that editors can't resist. Author Tom Williams wrote this special report on the basis of his years of experience handling free-lance submissions as editor and publisher of regional magazines and books and from his own successful free-lancing career. You won't learn this from other books and manuals. It's straight from the editor's desk. "It's so obvious," says Tom Williams, "yet I can count on one hand the number of queries containing these elements that cross my desk in a year's time." You'll love this one. It will get you published and put money in your bank account.

Venture Press. $14.95.

1011 How to Make Money Publishing Real Estate Guides and Apartment Directories
by Thomas A. Williams

You will earn big bucks from your real estate guide as a sideline or as a major enterprise. This *complete operations manual* reveals every single detail of building a highly profitable real estate publication, including organization, market analysis and positioning, publication design, distribution and sales organization and management. There's no need to spend big bucks for a franchise when you can get the inside knowledge you need from a publisher who has done it all. Perfect for moonlighting writers, self-publishers, salespersons and printers. *How to Make Money Publishing Real Estate Guides and Apartment Directories* openly reveals key trade secrets such as:

- How to start your business without the need for capital.
- How to recruit great salespeople at price you can afford.
- How to organize a sales campaign that will work, issue after issue.
- How to create powerful layout and design, even when you have no experience.
- How to analyze and overcome any competition.
- How to distribute your guide so that your clients get results and buy more advertising.

Step-by-step, easy-to-follow instructions enable you to set up your own publishing business. This book alone can double or triple your present income.

Venture Press. $39.95

1012 The Article Format That Always Sells
by Thomas A. Williams

When the wolf is knocking at the door, write one of these. Editors love these short and meaty pieces that make money or solve problems for their readers. But they must be formatted according to the desired formula. Follow a few simple rules and these easy to write articles will make you a successful, published—frequently published—author. Sale after sale will be yours as you build a valuable reputation in your field. This format is a favorite of savvy, experienced freelancers yet can be easily handled by the beginner. Great ideas abound. You'll never be stuck for them again. The opportunity is there, too. Says one editor, "As an editor of a general interest magazine, I was amazed at how few of this kind of article I was queried on. I was ready to buy them, but no one was turning them out.

Venture Press $14.95

For Immediate Shipment, Call (919) 975-2066

Writer's Warehouse & Self-Publisher's Supply
104 South Respess Street
Washington, NC 27889
(919) 975-2066

1022 How to Save Money on Your Taxes: Tax Tips and Tax Shelters for Freelance Writers and Self-Publishers
by Thomas A. Williams

Keep the money in your own pocket and out of IRS coffers. How to qualify as a business. A guided tour through those fabulous deductions for freelancers and self publishers. Learn about those tax deductible vacations and weekend trips. Let Uncle Sam help pay for your books and magazines. Find out about the advantages of incorporating your writing or publishing business. Save big bucks by paying some living expenses and health care out of pre-tax dollars. How to keep the records you need to claim the deductions you've got coming. Contains reproducible forms you will need to document your claims.

Venture Press. Ringbound. $14.95.

1023 **1001 Ways to Market Your Books,**
by John Kremer

This book describes over 1000 ideas, tips and suggestions for marketing books . It is a treasure chest of ideas. Many of them you will use as is, others will trigger special applications in your mind that will apply perfectly to your book project. An extremely valuable resource for anyone selling books.

"Kremer...knows his subject, imparting important information in a fast-paced, very open way. Good stuff here." - *The Book Reader*.

448 pages with bibliography and index. $19.95, hardcover.

1024. **Book Publishing Resource Guide**
by John Kremer

The *Book Pubishing Resource Guide* is a a directory of key contacts for marketing and promoting books., including:

- 212 distributors and 380 jobbers
- 147 publishers who distribute books
- 488 wholesalers
- 182 book clubs
- 305 mail order catalogues that feature books
- 102 bookselling and publishing associations
- 787 magazines that review books.
- 249 publicity and marketing services

320 pages, softcover. $25.00

ORDER BLANK
Satisfaction Guaranteed

☎ Telephone Orders: Call (919) 975-2066. Have your credit card ready.

✉ Postal Orders: Writer's Warehouse (919) 975-2066
104 South Respess Street, Washington, NC 27889

Item	Price
Subtotal	
Tax (5%)	
Shipping	
Total Enclosed	

Ship to:
Firm name: _____

Your name: _____

Address: _____

City: _____ State: _____ Zip: _____

Telephone: (   ) _____

Payment: ❑ Check   ❑ Credit Card

Expiration Date: _____

Please charge my ❑ Visa   ❑ MasterCard

Card Number: _____

Name on Card: _____

Signature: _____

Shipping:
$2.00 for the first book at $1.00 for each additional book or $3.00 each for Air Mail.

Sales Tax:
Add 5% sales tax.

For Immediate Shipment, Call (919) 975-2066

Writer's Warehouse & Self-Publisher's Supply
104 South Respess Street
Washington, NC 27889
(919) 975-2066